101
CONTRARIAN
IDEAS
ABOUT
ADVERTISING

The Strange World of Advertising

in 101 Delicious Bite-Size Pieces

BOB HOFFMAN

Author of "The Ad Contrarian"

ISBN 978-0-9796885-4-6 (print version)

Table of Contents

i   Foreword

iii   Author's Notes

1   Chapter 1
The Business of Advertising

33   Chapter 2
The Art of Advertising

59   Chapter 3
Cranky Advice and Opinions

79   Chapter 4
The Digital Dream World

119   Chapter 5
Brand Babble and Marketing Madness

151   Chapter 6
Myths and Magic

181   Chapter 7
The Advertising Follies

203   Chapter 8
Contrariana

223   Acknowledgements

225   About the Author

Foreword

First of all, you owe me two contrarian ideas. I promised 101 but there are actually 103 in this book.

I'm not going to be a dick about this, so if you don't have two ideas to send me, you can send me two bucks or something. How about two bottles of Ketel One? Whatever seems fair.

Now that we've gotten your obligations out of the way, let's talk about the book.

It's mostly stuff I wrote for my blog *The Ad Contrarian*. In almost five years of writing *The Ad Contrarian* blog, I've published over 1,000 pieces. Most of them were pretty stinky, but there were a few good ones and I think they're nicely represented in this collection.

The difficult part of writing the blog was that I toiled mercilessly and received not a penny. It's payback time. You want to read something about advertising that isn't the usual brain-liquefying drivel? This time you're going to pay.

There are some pieces in the book that are not about advertising. They're about things like fish and cosmology and singing our national anthem. I have called it *101 Contrarian Ideas About Advertising* because I thought *101 Contrarian Ideas About Advertising And Fish And Cosmology And Singing Our National Anthem* sounded stupid. I think you'll agree.

I have spent more time than is healthy in the ad business. During my unbecoming longevity, I have developed a deep and abiding cynicism—not so much for the ads themselves but for the way in which the ad business is conducted. It has been my experience that bad advertising gets punished by the market, but bad advertising business practices are thriving as never before.

One advertising blog called my last book (also called *The Ad Contrarian*) "the best ad book of the last 10 years." They have since, on several occasions, tried to take it back, but I have it in writing, so they can't. Ha!

I like to think of this new book as "the best ad book of the last 10 minutes." I realize it's not a *great* accolade, but at least it's something.

Anyhow, I hope you enjoy it. And if you don't, write your own damn book.

By the way, the three funniest words in the English language are nympho, homo, and Kotex.

Author's Notes

A handful of these pieces first appeared in *Adweek* magazine. The rest come from my blog, *The Ad Contrarian*. In order to avoid repetition and make the book more readable, in some cases I have combined pieces. In others, I have done some surgery. Since the material first appeared some of the data cited have changed. For the sake of accuracy I have left most of the data as they were at the time the pieces were first published.

Chapter 1
The Business of Advertising

ROBBIE AND RUTHIE TALK ABOUT PICKLES

The phone rings:

ROBBIE Hello.

RUTHIE Robert, it's your Aunt Ruthie.

ROBBIE Hi Ruthie.

RUTHIE Hello, darling.

ROBBIE What's up?

RUTHIE I'm calling to ask a favor.

ROBBIE Sure.

RUTHIE My pickles are selling very well, and Big Save says they'll put them in their supermarkets all across the country, but I have to do some advertising. So I thought as long as my nephew is a big shot advertising man, maybe your company could make an ad for me.

ROBBIE Sure.

RUTHIE So here's what I want the ad to say . . . Aunt Ruthie's Pickles are homemade, they taste wonderful and we use fresh ingredients.

ROBBIE Well, okay, but we really need to think a little more about this.

RUTHIE Um . . . okay . . . what?

ROBBIE Well, first we need to understand the consumer.

RUTHIE The consumer?

ROBBIE It's a . . . a person who buys things.

RUTHIE Everyone buys things.

ROBBIE Right . . .

RUTHIE So how is a consumer different from a person?

ROBBIE Um . . . it's not

RUTHIE So why don't you just call it a person?

ROBBIE Okay, so it's a person.

RUTHIE Okay so you have to understand this . . . person. Why?

ROBBIE So we can know how they use your product.

RUTHIE They eat it. How else do you use a pickle?

ROBBIE Well, yeah . . . but why do they eat it?

RUTHIE Because it tastes good. (PAUSE) Robbie, are you okay?

ROBBIE I'm fine. You see, we have to analyze who we should be talking to in our advertising. We call that a target audience. Should we talk to women 18–49 or men 25–34 or . . . ?

RUTHIE Why don't we just talk to people who like pickles?

ROBBIE Well you see, the perception of your brand has to resonate...

RUTHIE My what?

ROBBIE Your brand . . . it's the personality of your product . . .

RUTHIE My pickles have a personality?

ROBBIE Well, it's not the pickles that have the personality, it's you, it's *Aunt Ruthie's* Pickles . . .

RUTHIE My personality? I'm a pain in the ass. Why the hell does anyone care about my personality?

ROBBIE But Aunt Ruthie's is your brand.

RUTHIE I thought Aunt Ruthie was my name.

ROBBIE And your name is your brand!

RUTHIE So why don't you just call it my name? (PAUSE) Robert, are you having that problem you had back in college?

ROBBIE You know I've committed to never doing that again...

RUTHIE So why are you talking like this? Is this how you talk in your company?

ROBBIE Well, yes. You see, Aunt Ruthie, we believe advertising isn't really about selling your pickles. It's about developing a relationship between the consumer and your brand through integrated communications that create brand advocates by over-delivering on relevant brand expectations and engaging brand conversations . . .

RUTHIE You know, honey, your cousin Stanley majored in English. Maybe I'll just ask him to write the ad...

ROBBIE No, no . . . I'll . . .

RUTHIE Robbie, darling, you know I love you, right? And I would never say anything to hurt you. But listen to me, darling. You people are crazy.

Click

ADVERTISING'S FINAL SOLUTION

Good news!

We no longer need creative people in advertising.

We can finally get rid of those annoying, whiney, pains-in-the-ass.

According to *The New York Times* there's a new software program developed by an agency called *BETC Euro RSCG* that can generate advertising by itself.

But before we get to the software, let's talk about the agency for a minute.

Does an agency really need eight initials? I mean, the whole name is only twelve letters long—*BETC Euro RSCG*. And eight of them are initials. Maybe they should have used their software program to generate a better name.

Well, anyway, according to the *Times,* this program can create up to 200,000 "perfectly acceptable" ads for print, billboards, or banners. This sounds to me like an improvement because, honestly, I've seen a lot of banner ads that were perfectly awful, but I don't think I've seen many that were perfectly acceptable.

Now that computers can write and design ads, we can get down to the real business of advertising—you know, meetings and downloads and uploads and briefings and off-sites and Powerpoints and metrics and brand audits and deep dives.

We don't have to pretend we're in a "creative" business anymore. We can just do the things we're good at—imitation anthropology, sidewalk psychology, strategy torturing, and data misinterpretation.

No more of this so-called "creativity" bullshit.

ADVERTISING IN THE AGE OF HYSTERIA

Would everyone please calm down?

We've just lived through the most hysterical decade since the first doomsday lunatic discovered you could make a nice buck proclaiming the end of the world.

First, we had the Y2K bug. Everything was going to come to a grinding halt because . . . I don't know, something about software in clock radios. People were hoarding food and water.

Then there was the parade of pandemics that would kill us all—mad cow and SARS and bird flu and Ebola and swine flu. People were walking around airports in surgical masks (which, honestly, I would like to encourage).

Then there were killer bees and super-bacteria and sudden unintended acceleration and . . .

So, you're thinking, what does all this hysteria have to do with advertising? Well, if there's one thing we ad hacks understand it's the relationship between anxiety and cash flow. We've spent decades creating anxiety in consumers by convincing them that unless they had the latest $300 jeans they were in danger of social exile.

Now we can apply the same principles to our clients. And so we have created an ongoing hysteria-fest called *The Thing That Will Change Everything.* The object is to keep marketers in a constant state of anxiety about the future.

The more we can convince them that everything is changing around them—and they need us to interpret the changes—the longer we stay employed.

Consequently, every few months we come up with a new *Thing That Will Change Everything* to make them nice and jumpy. We've had practice at this. At one time we decided videotape was going to change everything. We'd be able to shoot spots in the morning (for $50) and have them on the air that afternoon.

Then the videocassette recorder was going to change everything. People would tape their favorite shows and play them back at their convenience (sound familiar?). And worst of all, they would fast-forward through the commercials (sound familiar?). Naturally, hysteria ensued.

Then the Web was going to change everything. Brick and mortar was dead and buried. The Web was going to create "disintermediation," which meant we would purchase all our cat food and pick-up trucks online, directly from the manufacturer.

Then there was TiVo. Nobody was going to watch TV in real time. We would time-shift all our viewing and skip the commercials. Then came YouTube. We would watch all video online, also without the annoyance of advertising.

Between TiVo, YouTube, podcasts, widgets and social media, the pundit digerati have declared traditional advertising officially dead. I Googled "advertising is dead" recently and came up with over 10,000 citations.

Well, I'm sad to inform our gloomy chatterers that digital technology has not destroyed advertising. But it has presented a new generation of dubious prophets with a cornucopia of *Things That Will Change Everything*.

What makes all the hysteria so silly and unwarranted is how quickly consumers digest and adjust to "the future"—and how seamlessly it arrives.

We have a vision of "the future" as a startling new thing that will confuse and disorient us. You'd think by now we'd have learned that it doesn't work that way. Someone introduces something astonishing—a mobile phone with a touch screen that can surf the Web, shoot video, play music, take photos and make the bed—and in about three weeks we're ready for something new.

Marketers seem resolutely attached to the belief that technological advances always lead to large-scale disruptions in consumer behavior. They have conferences about it every two weeks.

In fact, consumers have developed a remarkable ability to incorporate amazing technological changes into their lives with very little disruption to their purchasing habits. Of course, in every generation there actually *are* a few technological game-changers, like iTunes, but they are the rare, rare exception.

One of the untold stories of the digital age is the surprising degree to which consumer behavior has remained stable in light of a revolution in technology, communication and media.

A few examples:

- According to the U.S. Department of Commerce, e-commerce accounted for 4.1 percent of retail purchasing in Q2 2010. Brick-and-mortar retailing still represents about 96 percent of consumer activity.

- A study done at Duke University (with the cooperation of TiVo, IRI and in association with the University of Chicago) and released in May showed that even households with TiVo watch 95 percent of their TV live. Professor Carl Mela, who led the study, said, *"Our initial goal was to simply measure how bad DVRs were for advertisers . . . We tried a vast array of methodological approaches to find a DVR effect. And we just couldn't . . . find [any] change in people's shopping patterns when we compare a group that has TiVo with a group that doesn't."*

- Nielsen's Three Screen Report for the first quarter of 2010 shows that 99 percent of video is still viewed on a television. 1 percent is viewed online. Mobile viewing accounts for two-tenths of 1 percent of all video viewing. In other words, it essentially doesn't exist.

The marketing industry still hasn't gotten the memo that innovations in technology and media do not inexorably lead to major changes in consumer behavior. Over and over again, the facts tell us that these new technologies create small to moderate changes in purchasing behavior.

So why are we so enthusiastically supportive of the myth of *The Thing That Will Change Everything?* Simple. It's the Age of Hysteria. Keeping our clients in a state of anxiety is just plain good business.

EINSTEIN ON ADVERTISING

Albert Einstein was a pretty smart guy.

What most people don't know about Einstein is that in addition to uncovering the laws of relativity, the equivalency of mass and energy, and predicting that the speed of light was constant, he also said—without knowing it—the smartest thing ever said about advertising.

After his amazing successes as a young man, Einstein spent the rest of his life searching for what was called the "grand unified theory"—a theory that would unify the four known forces of nature: gravity, electro-magnetism, the strong nuclear force, and the weak nuclear force. Physicists believed—and most still do—that these four forces must be different manifestations of one underlying force.

Einstein worked for forty years on this problem and failed in his attempts to uncover a grand unified theory. To date, no one has found it.

Near the end of his life he was being interviewed. The interviewer asked Einstein if he thought a grand unified theory would ever be found. He said, "The answer to this problem, when found, will be simple."

No matter how complex a marketing or advertising problem seems to be; no matter how much research has been done; no matter how many conflicting opinions there are; no matter how many account planning insights have been concocted; no matter how many decks have been written, and Powerpoint presentations have been made, remember what Uncle Albert said—the correct idea, when found, will be simple.

EXTREMELY GOOD AT SOMETHING SPECIFIC

An interesting piece appeared in *Adweek* recently entitled, *In The Shadow of the Founders.*

The thrust of the piece is that it is often difficult for agencies to survive the exit of a charismatic founder.

The piece spotlights the troubles that have dogged agencies like Riney, Fallon, and Cliff Freeman as the founders have either left or taken reduced roles.

Of course, it is true that the exit of a charismatic founder often creates big problems for an agency. The thrust of the piece, however, misses the core of the issue.

The piece suggests that among the key prescriptions for a successful transition from charismatic founder to second generation, is that the new leadership has to share the values, principles, and culture of the founder.

This has almost nothing to do with it.

The reason charismatic agency leaders become successful in the first place is that they are usually extremely good at something specific. In other words, they have a talent.

They may be extremely good creative people, or extremely good strategists, or sales people, or extremely driven, or extremely confidence-inspiring.

To an outsider—and even to themselves—their success may seem to be related to values, principles, and culture. In fact, these usually emerge as a by-product of the success, not a cause.

That's why, when global agencies buy entrepreneurial agencies, and the founders leave, the globals almost always screw it up. They bring in a manager chock full of "values, principles, and culture" instead of someone who is extremely good at something specific.

HOW TO SELL GREAT CREATIVE WORK

The Big Show

You've been working on a new campaign for six weeks. Tomorrow's the day you present to the client.

The account director has booked the main conference room. Pastries have been ordered. The agenda has been Xeroxed.

Coming from the client organization are the CMO, the marketing director, the advertising manager, the brand manager and assistant brand manager, and maybe someone from upper management.

From the agency, the following people will be there: the account director, the account supervisor, the account executive, the executive creative director and/or creative director, the copywriter, art director, planning director and/or planner, media director, and maybe someone from upper management.

Already, you have no chance. None. You're dead meat. *The Grapes Of Wrath* couldn't survive this meeting. *Hamlet* couldn't survive it.

Large group presentations are the *death* of good advertising. Here's why:

- When you gather so many people together, the importance of the meeting becomes exaggerated.
- When a meeting takes on exaggerated importance, participants become anxious.
- Clients can *smell* agency anxiety a mile away. It's contagious and it causes fear. Fear is the enemy of an open mind.
- The meeting becomes a medium for the creation of subtle power relationships and a showcase for lower level people to demonstrate their analytic abilities (which is another way of saying 'finding flaws.')
- Every idea has weak points. *Moby Dick* has weak points. *The Great Gatsby* has weak points. People will be scrambling to show off by being the first to identify the weak points.
- Internal rivalries will be played out through the language of criticism.

- All comments will be irrelevant until the highest-ranking person speaks.

The biggest killer of good ideas is not research or clients or budgets. It's *The Big Show*.

In order to sell great work, you must do everything in your power to avoid *The Big Show*. You must avoid the conference room. You must avoid pastries and agendas.

Let's Do It On The Floor

At one point in my career I was creative director for the U.S. operation of an Australia-based agency called Mojo.

Mojo was recognized as one of the world's really good creative shops. At one point while I was there it was named "International Advertising Agency of the Year" by *Advertising Age*. It was ultimately bought by Jay Chiat and re-christened Chiat/Day/Mojo.

During my tenure there I learned a very important lesson about presenting creative work from Alan (Mo) Morris and Allan (Jo) Johnston.

Mo and Jo were unpretentious oddballs. They had a dread of big meetings, fancy presentations, and anything that smacked of formality. They shared an office and worked as a creative team, although they were both copywriters.

They had a very unusual and successful method of presentation. When they had an idea, they would call the real decision maker (more about this below) at the client company and invite him (usually a man in those days) over to the agency.

It would be Mo, Jo and the big guy. No account people, no researchers, no observers. They would sit in their office and spread the layouts or storyboards out on the floor, and then they'd explain the ideas.

No big set-ups. No Powerpoint. No parsing every word of the brief. None of the tortured logic of account planning. None of the usual agency rituals that turn creative presentations into torment and agony.

It removed all the major obstacles to a successful presentation:

- the anxiety of the big show
- the focus on the unimportant
- playing to the crowd
- the irrelevant opinions of onlookers

Their technique was very successful, and it helped them sell what they wanted to sell. It is without question a better way to accomplish the primary goal of both agency and client—to produce better advertising.

And yet, because of the structure and politics of most client-agency relationships, this method of operation is almost impossible.

Ego and Failure

At every client organization there is one person who is the *real decision maker.* In some companies it's the CMO. In some companies it's the CEO. In some companies it's the brand manager. Their title is irrelevant. The real decision maker is the person who can say "yes, go do it" *without having to show it to anyone else.*

At every agency, there is one person who is the *real creative leader* on the account. On some accounts it's the executive creative director. On some accounts it's the art director. On some accounts it's the president of the agency. Their title is irrelevant. The *real creative leader* is the person the *real decision maker* trusts and looks to for guidance.

The best creative work happens when the *real decision maker* and the *real creative leader* have a good relationship and work closely together.

The worst creative work is always the result of layers of people supervising layers of people.

Working in a marketing department is a tough job. The hours are grueling. The work is tedious. The finance, operations, and sales people think you're a bozo. You're always having to justify your budget. But there is a little fun—you get to attend creative presentations.

Working in an account services or creative department at an agency is a tough job. The work is frustrating. The client always has you on the defensive. But there is a little fun—you get to attend creative presentations.

Because marketing departments and agencies are difficult and frustrating places to work, and because agencies and clients want to keep their people happy, these people have been given an entitlement—they can come to creative presentations.

Packing the room with client and agency people just makes the process tougher. But it's essentially impossible for an agency manager to tell an account director or a creative director, "I don't want you in the presentation." It's virtually impossible for a CMO to say to a brand manager, "You really don't need to be there."

Egos simply can't tolerate this.

If you are an agency that wants to do good work on an account, someone in your creative department has to develop a good working relationship with the *real decision maker* on that account.

If you are a client that wants good creative work, you've got to undo the entitlements, and let the *real decision maker* at your company work directly with the *real creative leader* on your account.

After 100 years in the agency business, I still have no idea how to create great ads. It's a code I haven't cracked. But I do know how to sell them. Get your *real creative leader* together with their *real decision maker*, and get everyone else out of the fucking way.

ORDER AND CHAOS IN ADVERTISING

We exist in a world of delusions.

Our delusions live inside us and color everything we do. They infect our opinions of who we are. They distort our place in the world, twist our behaviors, and warp our sense of reality.

Like the proverbial fish in the ocean, we are so immersed in delusions we can't even sense they are there.

An article in last week's *New York Times* reminds us that we are very good at filtering out information that does not fit neatly into our vision of the world. "We can't cope otherwise" says James Glieck, author of books about chaos theory (and the famous "butterfly effect") and biographies of Newton and Feynman.

The business of advertising is particularly rife with delusions. We think we know how advertising works. We think we know what will motivate people and what will not. And yet, every day we unconsciously filter out compelling evidence that we don't really know anything.

After months of "research" and "testing" we create TV spots that have no effect. After hundreds of thousand of dollars in development we launch websites and online campaigns that no one ever sees. And yet we continue.

We go into new business presentations and make bold, cocksure statements about our own particular brand of delusional advertising philosophy. And we never have the guts or self-assurance to tell the truth—that all our posturing is just an estimate of likelihoods and a speculation on probabilities.

Part of it is our fault. We are not willfully deceitful. We just find it very hard to admit that we are devoting so much of our energy and our soul to something about which we really understand so little.

Part of it is the environment. Our clients want results. They don't want to hear that they are spending millions of dollars on likelihoods and probabilities.

Advertising is chock full of contingencies and unintended effects.

There are a multitude of critical steps in the development of advertising. None of which assures success. Every one of which can foreshadow failure.

Something as routine as the casting of a model for a photo shoot can have an enormous effect on the success or failure of a campaign. And that is just one of dozens of weighty variables. We cannot possibly assess all the variables in a methodical way. So we fall back on our prejudices and our mathematical models of how advertising works. In other words, we call forth our delusions.

The workings of the real world are impossibly complex and messy. And in advertising, as in every other human endeavor, as Glieck says, we "prefer to turn a blind eye to reality's messiness."

QUANTUM ADVERTISING

Quantum theory makes scientists crazy. It's the only area of science in which the idea of cause and effect (or, as they like to say, "deterministic causality") has to be suspended. One of the consequences of quantum theory is that in certain cases things just pop into and out of existence. In fact, there are physicists who believe our whole universe is a quantum event—it just appeared out of nothing for no reason.

Even Einstein, whose work laid the foundation for quantum physics, hated the idea. And yet it's the best and only explanation science has for a ton of phenomena that occur at the atomic and sub-atomic scale.

I'm starting to believe in quantum advertising. I think there are things that just happen for no reason. I've seen ad campaigns that are brilliant, strategically perfect, and beautifully produced fail miserably. I've seen stupid, ill-conceived campaigns work miraculously. Sometimes, all our logic just doesn't work.

I've seen agencies with tremendous experience in a category get a new account in that category and make a pig's breakfast out of it. I've seen the world's dumbest agencies get accounts they had no right to win and succeed wildly with awful, insight-free advertising.

It's uncomfortable for us to believe that success and failure in business are sometimes random and happen in spite of our efforts. We've been taught to look for reasons. But I guess if a whole universe can appear for no good reason, the odd marketing success can, too.

THE AMAZING INVISIBLE TIVO EFFECT

"...advertisers and television programmers must devise new strategies for combating the potentially disastrous effects of ad skipping."

— Jupiter Media

No technological development has created more hysteria and hand-wringing in the ad industry than the adoption of the DVR.

Over the past few years, the science department here at *Ad Contrarian* World Headquarters has tried to counterbalance the intemperate ravings of pundits and hysterical lunatics by introducing some facts and perspective into the discussion.

In my most recent post on the subject I calculated that as a result of time-shifting and ad-skipping only about 3% of total spots were being missed. A recent study, however, leads me to believe that this may be a gross exaggeration.

In fact, the true number may be as little as 1.2%.

In a 3-year study by Duke University in partnership with Information Resources Inc. (IRI), TiVo, and The University of Chicago, a sample of 1,588 households were studied to see, among other things, how they used their DVRs.

What made this study different from other research done on DVR usage was that it measured actual behavior, not self-reported behavior. As you know, self-reported behavior is highly suspect and almost always turns out to be inaccurate.

According to Duke, the results of the study ". . . astonished the researchers."

One of the key findings of the study was that 95% of the time people with DVRs were watching live TV. Only 5% of the time did they watch time-shifted TV.

If this is true, the number of total spots being missed as a result of ad-skipping is ridiculously small.

Let me explain in simple terms in case any art directors are reading this.

About 35% of households have DVRs. If they're time-shifting 5% of the time, then the total amount of programming being time shifted is 1.7% (5% of 35%.) If they skip 70% of ads while time shifting, then the total percent of spots being missed is 1.2% (70% of 1.7%.)

Now remember, TiVo was first introduced in 1998. While all the wailing and panic about DVRs has been going on, TV viewership has increased. As a matter of fact, according to Nielsen, TV viewership has increased 21% since 1998.

So, if the Duke study is correct, here's where we stand 12 years after the introduction of TiVo. DVRs are causing people to miss 1.2% of TV ads. Meanwhile, greater viewership is causing them to watch 21% more TV ads.

The positive effect of more viewing is almost 20 times the negative effect of the DVR.

THE CRISIS OF ADVERTISING

Advertising pundits are right about one thing. The ad industry is a mess. They are wrong, however, about what is causing the problems.

The crisis is not being caused by the internet. The internet should be a boon to advertising. The crisis is not being caused by "new media." New media should be stimulating a creative resurgence.

The crisis is not the result of consumers becoming immune to advertising. The idea that there is a new species of human that is suddenly not influenced by media is nonsense.

Unfortunately, the causes of the crisis are much deeper and intractable. They revolve around three factors.

1. Consolidation of the ad industry
2. Talent and brain drain
3. Mindless me-too-ism

Consolidation

There is one thing that the last 10 years has taught us about consolidation in service industries. Whether it's advertising or airlines, retailing or telecommunication, consolidation has become a service nightmare for customers.

The startling thing is that airline customers get it. Retail customers get it. Phone company customers get it. But, for the most part, clients of global ad agencies still don't get it.

Any survey of marketing companies makes it clear that they have lost confidence in ad agencies' abilities to positively affect their businesses. Yet they continue to hire the same five global agency networks over and over.

Not that long ago, Y&R had the largest share of market among advertising agencies at about 1.5%. Today five global behemoths control as much as 75% of advertising in America. Ask people in the trenches who work for one of these monstrosities and 90% of the time you will hear how dysfunctional and corrupt they have become.

Advertising was at its best when it was run by the entrepreneurs who were the "founding fathers" of the modern era. They started agencies because they thought they could do it better. They were mainly craftsmen—copywriters, art directors, and account guys—who had three goals: 1) to get out from under the thumbs of those who ran the dull agencies they were working at, 2) to make some money, 3) to make good ads.

Let's not be overly romantic here. The founding fathers (and a few founding mothers) of modern advertising were no less interested in making money than today's worldwide fat boys. However, they lived in a different world—a world in which making money in advertising was a by-product. It came from making good ads.

They were interesting people. Not every one was George Lois or David Ogilvy, but for the most part they were not the stupefyingly dull men in gray suits that run today's global ad corporations.

Today's publicly traded behemoths are lead by lawyers, accountants and financiers who could no more recognize a good ad than replace a carburetor. If their agencies never had to make another ad—if they could just be consultants and brand babblers—they'd be perfectly happy.

I am not naive enough to believe that the past was always better than today or that small is always better than big. And the ad industry has invariably had its share of con men, empty suits, and bullshit artists. However, having lived through it, I can tell you this—the conglomeratized ad industry of today, compared to what it used to be, is nothing to be proud of.

Talent

At one point in my career I left the agency business for three years and did creative work directly for clients. During those three years I learned a very important lesson about ad agencies. Clients do not like working with us.

They mostly laugh (behind our backs) at our supposed strategic abilities. They see very little value in what we call "account service."

They believe they can get media planning done anywhere.

They put up with us for one reason and one reason only. We're their only source for creativity. Or at least we have been.

A very significant part of the crisis we are facing is that talented young creative people used to strive to work in advertising. They no longer do. And if we don't have creativity to sell, we got nothin'.

At the beginning of this piece I stated that *"The crisis is not being caused by the internet. The internet should be a boon to advertising."* There is, however, one way in which the ascendancy of the web is harming ad agencies. We are allowing it to draw off a whole generation of talented creative people.

Not long ago, young people with creative talent had three options.

First, they could go into fine arts. They could write novels or plays. If they were visual artists they could go into painting or sculpture. If they were musicians they could play or compose serious music.

Second, if they were talented but not quite brilliant, they could go into the popular arts: writing for tv or movies, pop music, or popular art.

Third, if they were talented but couldn't make it in the world of fine art or popular art, there was commercial art, including advertising. (I know. Gross generalizations. Obviously, there have been some brilliant commercial artists and some terrible "fine" artists. In general, however, it is true that there is a hierarchy of fine art, popular art, and commercial art.)

The web has changed this in two ways. For one thing, it is now possible to bypass the standard routes to creative success. Talented people who previously had no access to channels of artistic exposure can now show their work on the internet at a cost of about zero.

Next—and most critical to us in the ad business—working in digital media has become far more attractive to them than working in traditional advertising.

A great many talented young people who in the past would have been drawn to advertising are now choosing to create for the web.

And they are not creating ads for the web. They are creating websites, games, social networks, blogs, videos, and all manner of oddball hybrids. They have an alternative to what we used to consider commercial art.

Put yourself in the place of a young, talented person. You can work for a big, clumsy ad agency that is toiling for huge corporations and have dozens of knuckleheads sticking their sweaty fingers into everything you do, or you can work for yourself, or a smaller entity, where you don't just use your imagination to sell things, you use it to actually create things.

The ad industry is not attracting these talented young people like it used to. And it needs them desperately.

If we cannot provide clients with the one thing they really want from us—creativity—there is little future for the ad industry as it is currently configured.

Brain Drain

The following is a true story.

One of our junior account people was hired by one of our clients. She had done a nice job working on the account. The client, not understanding the difference between *cooks and waiters*, hired her to be their advertising manager.

Within a month, this woman—who had essentially been an amiable delivery person and had never been within fifty yards of an ad or a strategy—was telling our account director what our strategies should be, telling our creative director how our ads should look, and threatening our tenure on the account.

Is it any wonder smart, ambitious marketing people are getting harder to recruit into agency account management?

These days, you have to really love advertising to be in account management. When things go well, it's because the creatives are brilliant. When things go badly, you screwed up.

You have no time to do your job because you're usually doing your client's job.

You have little say over strategy. Account planners and creative directors are busy screaming at each other over that. Your only responsibility is to keep them from killing each other.

Worst of all, you can never adequately explain to your mother what the hell it is you actually do.

Is this what you got a business degree for?

A lot of people don't think so. That's why the agency business is not attracting the type of marketing talent we need. Talented account people are now just as hard to hire as talented creative people.

There are several factors underlying the exodus of smart people from account management.

The tactical always drives out the strategic: Clients have lost discipline, patience and focus. They are unwilling to stay with any idea for more than six months. This drives strategic thinkers crazy.

Who's got authority? Client-side marketing people have been given grander titles and less authority. Agencies will work for months on strategies approved by CMOs, only to have them ripped to shreds at the last minute by the real decision makers. This, too, drives smart people crazy.

Account planning: Responsibility for marketing strategy used to be in the hands of account managers. It no longer is. (Concurrently, there has been a general loss of confidence among clients in ad agencies' abilities to provide strategic guidance. Maybe it's a coincidence, but this loss of confidence has correlated almost perfectly with the ascendancy of account planning.)

Self-respect: Many high-level account managers are directed by client-side people they wouldn't hire to be their assistants.

Account management has always been a thankless and difficult job. Traditionally, however, smart account managers could get satisfaction by strongly influencing their clients' business strategies. They once provided clients with insights into the hard sciences of sales and marketing. Today, agencies are less interested in sales and marketing than they are in the soft science of cultural anthropology.

Ambitious marketing people want no part of it. I don't blame them.

What To Do

I've written three drafts of this and I still don't know what the hell I'm trying to say. The Crisis of Advertising? I have no idea what to do about it and anyone who says he does is full of baloney.

The first draft I wrote said we were going the way of the music industry, *i.e.,* evaporating. That's just simply not going to happen.

The second draft said that BDAs (big dumb agencies) were going to turn into black holes, exploding under the gravitation of their own mass. That's not going to happen either.

So here are some random thoughts about how the agency business needs to change, how you as an agency or you as an individual might want to think about what's next.

Contrary to all the nonsense you read, advertising is not dead. You can't swing a dead account planner without hitting an ad. They're everywhere—urinals, grocery check-out separators, dry cleaning bags. Advertising is thriving even though agencies aren't.

There just isn't enough value anymore in big, slow, expensive ad agencies. Smart, industrious clients can cobble together small groups to get the work done at less cost and with superior creativity. They just don't know it yet.

The most important client-side marketing job currently does not exist: Someone to coordinate the activities of a variety of small, nimble marketing and advertising resource providers.

The idea that global agencies can provide global marketing solutions is an idiotic fraud that anyone with the intelligence of a gnat should be able to see through. You can't find a single agency to get done everything you need in Los Angeles, how the hell are they supposed to do it worldwide? That global agencies even *exist* is a testament to the laziness of global marketers.

There will always be a place for BDAs because there will always be BDCs.

There will also be a place for regional, independent agencies because there will always be entrepreneurs and regional advertisers.

The middle, however, will continue to collapse. This will create big failures and enormous opportunities.

The web has turned us all into liars. We pretend the web has opened up huge new advertising opportunities when we secretly know that it has mostly been a dismal failure as an advertising medium. We cling to the few big successes and argue from the extreme. We pretend we know how to do it all, but we don't. We pretend to be "media neutral" but secretly we are either broadcast-centric, print-centric, or web-centric.

The strategic part of what agencies do is going to disappear. Smart clients have no confidence in account planning. Those who haven't yet, will soon take strategy away from agencies and place it in-house or in the hands of consultants.

All their baloney notwithstanding, the huge media buying conglomerates have commoditized media buying and it is becoming a price war.

The one and only leverageable asset agencies will be left with will be creativity. The definition of creativity has evolved into more than just making ads, and it will continue to evolve.

Agencies will try to create relationships with creative resources outside the industry (directors, writers, performers) and, as always, this will fail. You will need your own creative resources.

Here are some strategies to think about:

Specialize: Go against the grain. Every agency is trying to convince clients that they can do it all. Instead, be an agency that does only one thing really well. Specialize in retail, or become expert in marketing to Mid-Westerners, or only work on luxury brands, or only do creative work. Find something you can be famous for.

Get small and do it yourself: The economics of the ad industry are going to hell. It's hard to make money. Soon big agencies may realize they can be more profitable by outsourcing to smaller, nimbler entities. Become a small, nimble entity. Have your own clients and do contract work for BDA's.

Confederate: Form a confederated brand with other small, nimble entities. One does strategy. One does creative. One does media planning. One does promotions. You are independent, but you work cooperatively. You provide clients with a single service or a suite of services.

Something completely different: This is the most likely answer. The next model for the ad business is likely to be something we haven't even thought of.

Now is a perfect time to look at the ad industry in a new way. Throw away what you think you know. What are the big problems clients are facing? What's a new way to deliver solutions? Times of economic stress force companies to do something they hate — search for new answers.

This is a great time for new ideas and innovative thinking. Get off your ass and do something different.

10 IDEAS FOR TRANSFORMING ADVERTISING

Yesterday, I received the following email from the head of the *American Association of Advertising Agencies.*

Are You A Transformer?

> *Dear Bob,*
>
> *Like you, I'm tired of hearing from the same industry thought leaders talking about the same so-called thought-leading things at industry conferences. What I really want is to hear from you: If you had just five minutes in front of the entire advertising community, what would you say about transforming advertising as we know it?*
>
> *I've started a new program called 4A's Transformers, and we've just opened up our call for entries for anyone — inside or outside advertising — to share his or her transformational idea about advertising. For winning Transformers, we'll give you five minutes on the conference mainstage at Transformation 2010, our annual meeting, which will be held February 28 through March 3, 2010, at the Hilton San Francisco Union Square.*
>
> *What's the catch? There is no catch. I'll pick up the tab for your travel and hotel stay at the conference (roundtrip coach airfare and one night at the Hilton). All you need to do is dazzle me (and the 4A's Board of Directors) with your brilliant idea for transforming advertising.*
>
> *Deadline for entries is Tuesday, January 12, 2010. Click here for contest details.*
>
> *You've been blogging or twittering about what you'd do if you were in charge for years. Now's your chance! What are you waiting for?*

Here at *The Ad Contrarian* Global Headquarters, we always welcome a challenge. So here we go . . .

101 Ideas For Transforming Advertising

1. No cranberry bagels at meetings. No exceptions.
2. While on duty, copywriters required to wear those Peruvian knit hats with the funny earflaps.

3. Reinstatement of the three martini lunch. After a 6-month trial period, optional upgrade to four.

4. Confiscate all computers and baseball caps from art directors.

5. Use of the following terms will be considered justifiable cause for termination: ecosystem, conversation, engagement, landscape, seared ahi tuna, and quirky.

6. When making presentations, account planners must dress up as pirates and hop around on one foot.

7. Breakthrough idea for tv spots: Animals that talk!

8. Criminalize all products containing pomegranates or acai berries.

9. Increase touch points from 360 degrees to 380 degrees.

10. Require Sir Martin Sorrell to walk around with his weenie out.

Chapter 2

The Art of Advertising

WHY CREATIVES ARE ALWAYS CONFUSED

As you stroll the halls of an ad agency you often encounter people wearing baseball caps, wandering aimlessly and muttering to themselves.

We call these people "creatives." They are the ones who make the ads.

They are always confused. Here's why.

They are pressured by their leaders to do "great" work. But when they do, they usually get reprimanded for not being "on strategy."

They are encouraged to win awards. But when they do, they are dismissed as childish narcissists.

They are highly paid, but rarely listened to.

They are told that it's "all about the work" but come to learn that it's "all about the metrics" or "all about the relationship" or "all about the conversation" or "all about" whatever the cliche-of-the-month is.

When they say advertising is an art, their clients say it's a business.

When they say it's a business, their clients say it's an art.

When they finally get something good produced, it fails.

When they produce mundane crap, it works.

When their friends like it, their clients hate it.

When their clients like it, their friends hate it.

They are encouraged to be collaborative. But the more people touch their work, the worse it gets.

They are counseled against becoming prima donnas. But they see that the people who get good jobs are often disagreeable monsters.

If they weren't confused they'd be crazy.

THE 2 MOST IMPORTANT WORDS IN ADVERTISING

I've never been to ad school or art school.

I've never taken a course in copywriting or design.

I've never read a text book about marketing or strategy or account planning or media.

So I have no idea if what I'm about to say is commonly taught in classrooms and "how-to" advertising books, or if it's just some heresy I made up.

Creativity is very important in advertising. Strategy is very important in advertising. But, I'm sorry people, there is something much simpler and much more basic that is more important in producing persuasive ad copy.

It's this: Be specific.

There are a lot of good Italian restaurants in my neighborhood. But I go to one regularly because I love the bread.

My favorite pair of sneakers aren't the ones that look the nicest or absorb shock the best. They're the ones that are the widest.

My favorite recording isn't of the best song I ever heard, or have best vocal I ever heard, but it does have my favorite sax solo.

The point is—like most people—when I have a preference, it is usually for a very specific reason. And yet, throughout my career one of toughest things I have had to do is to convince my clients to be more specific.

Many have a hard time understanding that "we answer on the first ring" is a more powerful promise than "world class service."

They don't believe that "$50 off" is a stronger motivator than "we'll make your dreams come true."

Many have thought that the bigger and more ambiguous the promise, the bigger the payoff. It is usually the opposite. The more specific the promise, the more salient the proposition.

We have all seen advertising that is ugly and stupid succeed. We have all seen advertising that is lovely and intelligent fail. I would suggest to you that if you go back and look, you will find that the successful ugly and stupid advertising said something specific about the product and the unsuccessful lovely, intelligent advertising was full of platitudes and generalizations.

That's why horrible car dealer advertising is sometimes more effective than beautiful car manufacturer advertising.

The best advertising is strategically wise, creatively pleasing, and *specific*.

Perhaps my favorite example of this is the idea the iPod was launched with:

Not *"world class mp3 player."*

Not *"a whole new way to enjoy music."*

But this: *"A thousand songs in your pocket."*

"WHAT IS GOOD CREATIVE AND HOW DO I GET IT?"
A talk to a group of ad agency owners on the subject of creativity.

The subject matter of my talk this morning is "What is good creative work and how do I get it?"

My intent is to take us through a course of logic in the hope that at the end we will reach the discomforting conclusion that perhaps the lies we've been telling ourselves about creativity deserve more thought than we've given them.

Let's first rid ourselves of the notion that the definition of good creative work is simply "that which is successful in the marketplace." That definition is merely a tautology and doesn't tell us a thing about the nature of "good creative."

Good creative has certain characteristics.

- It is the stuff that is beautiful, or outrageous, or funny, or interesting.
- It is the stuff we wish we had done.
- It is advertising we would volunteer to watch.

We have a roomful of highly successful ad agency owners here today and I think it is mildly disingenuous of us to pretend that we don't know what good creative is.

I believe we all know what it is, but we make a game of finding esoteric definitions for it in order to justify what most of us produce most of the time—which is *not* good creative.

So we re-define what creativity means in order to deceive ourselves into thinking that what we're doing is good. We tell ourselves that creativity is, for example, "the clear and compelling articulation of a strategy". Which, in my opinion, is not creativity.

Creativity is unrelated to strategy. Let me say that again— creativity is unrelated to strategy.

Creativity is what happens *after* the strategy is done. Creativity is the process that transforms a strategy into a terrific ad. Or, more commonly, the absence of creativity is what transforms a strategy into a smelly turd.

That's not to say that strategy is not an important component of advertising. It is. It's just that advertising has two components. The first is strategy. The second is creativity.

Now before all you account guys start yapping at me, I stipulate that there is a "small c" creative component to the development of strategy and that the difference between an average strategy and an excellent one is often the degree to which it is creatively conceived.

However, I don't think that is what we're talking about here. When we talk about "creativity" in the context of advertising. What we're usually talking about is what the copywriter and art director do after the planners are finished mucking-up the brief.

In my opinion, those who think creativity is merely "the clear and compelling articulation of a strategy" are doomed to a career of apologizing—apologizing for mediocre ads, and apologizing for mediocre results.

Now the complicated part of all this—and the part that is guaranteed to drive you crazy—is that good creative doesn't always produce good business results. Which is another way of saying that good creative isn't always effective advertising. Why? Nobody knows. Sometimes it works, sometimes it doesn't.

Despite our many pretensions to the contrary, there's an awful lot we don't know about advertising. We get up in front of our clients and feed them a lot of hogwash about branding or engagement or whatever happens to be the contemporary buzzword of choice, and that's fine. They expect us to be full of shit. But I would strongly suggest that you don't start believing your own baloney or you'll find yourself in hot water pretty quick.

If you're going to be the type of agency that does good creative work, you're just going to have to get used to the idea that you usually can't prove that it's any better than doing crap. And you're going to have to get used to the idea that good creative sometimes fails.

On the other hand, if you're going to be the kind of agency that does not do good creative work, you're going to have to get used to always being on the defensive with your clients. And you're going to have to get used to the idea that even when bad creative succeeds, it is still stinky and you're still going to be apologizing for it.

Those are your unpleasant options.

Whichever course you choose, you can be sure you'll always be on the hot seat.

The way I see it, if you're going to be miserable anyway, you might as well be miserable doing good creative work.

The second part of the question is "How do I get creativity." The answer to that one is simple. You buy it.

Creativity is a rare and precious commodity. The reason there are so many crappy ads in the world is the same reason there are so many crappy books, and crappy songs, and crappy movies, and crappy TV shows. It's not because there's a conspiracy to create crappy stuff. It's just that creating good stuff is very difficult and there are very few people who can do it.

We have been told by new age charlatans that "we're all creative people" and that all we have to do is free ourselves from the artificial restraints of our society and our culture and all our creativity will flow forth.

Bullshit.

Creativity is the most rare and precious of commodities. It is the result of hard work, discipline, and above all, talent.

You can't teach talent. You can barely manage it. You have to go out and find it and buy it.

So, in 10 words or less:

- What is good creative? You know what it is.

- How do I get it? You buy it.

But those are the simple questions. The hard questions are: Do you really want creativity, and what are you willing to sacrifice to get it?

First of all, really good creative people are dangerous. Some clients don't like them. As a matter of fact, many clients don't like them.

I have seen agencies that have done terrible advertising for years suddenly produce a really good campaign. And get fired. Creativity is not for the timid.

Talented creative people are hard to find. Those who call themselves "creatives" in our business are, to a large extent, mediocrities who delude themselves into thinking that if they have a silly haircut and an annoying personality they must be talented.

The only thing that truly talented creative people have in common with the mass of not-very-talented creative people is that they, too, are pains in the ass.

Great creative people are smarter than us. They will challenge everything we say, they will scoff at the pathetic strategies we come up with, and they will make trouble and annoy the shit out of us.

They will also—under the right circumstances—make us rich and famous.

EMOTION IS A RESPONSE, NOT A STIMULUS

In the early to mid 90's, Toyota and General Motors shared a manufacturing facility in Fremont, California. The plant had a line that built the Toyota Corolla and the (Chevrolet) Geo Prizm. It was the same vehicle, built at the same facility, by the same people. At the end of the production line some cars got the Corolla badge and some got the Prizm badge.

At one point, the Corolla sold for $1,500 more. Yet it outsold the Prizm 3 to 1.

It is clear that if humans were logic machines, this could never happen. There is no logic that can explain this phenomenon. The only explanation is that Corolla carried an emotional value that Prizm did not.

It is an article of faith in the advertising and marketing world that some of the strongest bonds between consumers and brands are built on emotional attachments or beliefs. There is certainly a lot of truth in this.

The question for brands is, where does this emotional value come from and how do you get it?

The usual response to this question from advertisers is "emotion in, emotion out." That's why we get a certain type of advertising from insurance companies, banks, oil companies, and misguided marketers in dozens of other categories. You've seen these ads a thousand times—mothers cradling newborn babies; people in wheelchairs participating in marathons; parades down Main Street; grandpa playing catch with Timmy.

These are supposedly "emotional" moments that are meant to elicit emotional responses. What they actually are are warmed-over cliches that elicit nothing but yawns and trips to the toilet.

The fallacy behind this type of advertising is the assumption that the only way to elicit an emotional response is through images rather than logic.

I can see no reason why logical, benefit-oriented advertising should be any less capable of eliciting an emotional response, and an emotional attachment to a brand, than advertising that is fact-free, benefit-challenged and crassly emotionalistic.

I'll bet if you hooked people up to an emote-o-tron and measured responses, you'd find as much emotional response to "15 minutes can save you 15%" as you would to grandma baking cookies.

This is not to say that there haven't been very effective ads that have done a wonderful job at conveying emotion. There certainly have been. But they are a minuscule minority. Most that try for this fail miserably.

It is true that humans are not logic machines. But, remember, emotion is a response. Not a stimulus.

SMELLY VOLVO FAMILIES

I was at the movies last Saturday night and saw a remarkably ill-conceived theatrical spot for Volvo. It was a faux James Bond thing with yachts and helicopters and jet planes and very expensive looking people doing idiotic superhero things.

The gag, you see, was that these people were a married couple in different parts of the world trying to get together for their anniversary. It ended with some inanity about life being better together. A beautiful example of a spot written to justify a tag line. It had absolutely nothing to do with Volvo and had the tortured logic of account planning written all over it.

The theater was in Berkeley where there are more Volvos per capita than Stockholm. If Volvo had intentionally set out to alienate their customer base they couldn't have done a better job.

My daughter used to call them "smelly Volvo families." They drive beat-up 10-year old Volvo station wagons with Goldfish crumbs lodged in the folds of the upholstery, plastic milk crates in the back filled with old sneakers, and old "John Edwards for President" bumper stickers. The men all have some form of greying facial hair, the women have an unfortunate tendency to wear woven ponchos. At least one of them is a therapist. Very few of them hang out on yachts.

They drive a Volvo for the following reasons:

1. To show they are smarter than us.

2. To show they are immune to imagery and marketing.

3. To show they are more concerned with safety than style.

4. Oh, and did I mention they are smarter than us?

They will be appalled by this "new" Volvo.

Volvo is making a classic marketing mistake. They are trying to be someone else. Instead of positioning themselves as a new, safer, more stylish Volvo they are aiming to be the second best BMW.

I'm sure there's some marketing genius/account planner telling them that safety isn't enough and they have to make an "emotional bond" with consumers. This is typical marketing nonsense and TAC predicts that they will learn this the hard way. They have relinquished their unique reason for being.

SEVEN LESSONS FROM APPLE

The New York Times had a nice piece yesterday about how Apple has been kicking Microsoft's ass in advertising for about a thousand years.

Here are some lessons from that rivalry.

1. Apple's advertising is almost always about product benefits and differentiation. It is never idiotic "branding" like the Gates/Seinfeld atrocity. No lifestyle bullshit, just clear differentiation between its products and its rivals' products. And always done beautifully.

2. Apple knows who they are. Even though they have rivals with much larger market shares, they are assiduous in not trying to be like them. They are content to be who they are and don't pretend to be someone else. Their personality is clear, consistent and unapologetic. If you like us, great. If you don't, so be it. This is an important aspect of their strategy that most marketers are clueless about. It is never a good idea to try to be the second best Anything. It is far more compelling to be the best Something.

3. Steve knows good ads. Although I've never worked on any Apple business, I've heard that nothing important gets done without Steve Jobs' approval. It is essential that a client organization has someone who can recognize good advertising in its early stages. It is perfectly clear that most CMOs can't.

4. Bad names last forever. We are so used to the name Microsoft, we have forgotten what an alarmingly awful, cringe-inducing name it is. When you start with such bad taste, it's hard to ever recuperate.

5. Everything starts at the top. I'm willing to bet that Apple's marketing department is every bit as confused, screwed-up, and ineffectual as every other marketing department in America. The difference? They have Steve.

6. Great products make everyone a marketing genius.

7. Great agencies make everyone a marketing genius. Kudos to TBWA/Chiat/Day for its Apple work—the longest run of great advertising in the history of the sport.

One last lesson: as Microsoft clearly demonstrates, you don't have to make good advertising to be successful.

   Dammit.

CREATIVITY WITHOUT TALENT

Someone once asked me about a copywriter who had worked for me. "Is he creative?" the person asked. "Very" I replied, "and it's a shame because he's not very talented."

I, too, am burdened with this frustrating affliction—more creativity than talent.

I spend an inordinate amount of time writing and playing musical instruments. I love doing these things. But, alas, I'm just not very good at them.

I have written some decent ads, some pretty good blog posts, and some fairly lousy songs. But no one would accuse me of being terribly talented.

But this post isn't about me, it's about advertising.

We are often confronted with the lament that advertising isn't very good. This is true, and one of the reasons it's true is that the ad industry is chock full of people like me.

I've seen them from all sides. As a copywriter, I've worked alongside them. As a creative director I've supervised them. As an agency head, I've recruited them.

They are hard-working, diligent, and well-meaning. Unfortunately, they're not very talented. By definition, the average creative person is, well, average. And as George Carlin would remind us, half of them are below average.

We often blame the absence of excellence in advertising on tin-eared clients, unimaginative strategies, or weak-kneed account work. The truth, however, is a little more complicated.

Talent is a rare and precious thing. Every now and then I'll see a spot and it will blow me away, "Oh, so that's how you do it."

It's not that we don't want to do great work. It's not that we don't try to do great work. It's just that great work is really, really difficult to do. It takes exceptional talent, and sadly, exceptional talent is the exception.

ATTACK OF THE TALKING VAGINAS

There is an alarmingly awful series of commercial videos currently visible on YouTube for Summer's Eve.

The premise of this campaign is that your vagina (portrayed by a hand) is talking to you. Not being the proud owner of a vagina, it's hard for me to comment on the effect this campaign might have on someone who does have one. But from the verbal reaction I am getting from women, I don't think this campaign is making Summer's Eve any friends.

I'm sure the Summer's Eve people were not naive about the effect it would have. I am sure they understood that there was a significant portion of the population who would be offended by these videos, but they were willing to take the chance to get some attention.

While I think the decision was misguided, I can see how it might have paid off. It might have paid off if the campaign was funny; if it wasn't so poorly written and performed.

Back when I was a creative director I used to drive the people in my creative department crazy with the following criticism of their storyboards: This is not a spot. It's an idea. Now you need to make it into a spot.

What happened in this Summer's Eve travesty is that someone had an idea. The idea was that a "hand puppet" could substitute for a vagina and a vagina could talk. It's a pretty damn gross idea, but it's an idea.

In the hands of someone who could write, this idea might actually have been turned into something interesting. In the hands of the dullards who wrote and produced it, it is awful.

Regardless of what they did with it, Summer's Eve were going to offend some people. That's fine. The problem with this thing is, even the people who were not automatically going to be offended will be horrified because the writing and performances are so astonishingly dumb.

Comedy is a funny thing. It's easy to be funny over lunch. It's very hard to be funny standing up in front of a hundred people. It's the same in advertising. It's easy to have a funny idea. It's very hard to make a funny spot.

The Summer's Eve campaign had a very slight chance to be successful. It is stunningly unfunny, and as a result it is a disaster.

I don't hate this campaign because it's offensive. I hate it because it's done so witlessly.

SIX THINGS A CREATIVE DIRECTOR NEEDS TO KNOW

Here are six things you need to know if you're going to be a happy, healthy creative director.

1. *Hiring is everything.*

   If you have terrific people the advertising business isn't that difficult. If you have mediocrities advertising is impossible. For your own self-preservation you must get rid of bad people and hire good ones. There is no other way to do good work and have a happy life. The idea that "we're all creative" is absolute bullshit. Mediocre talent never makes terrific ads. Never.

2. *Avoid the "tyranny of strategy."*

   Strategies are not written by God. They are written by planners, researchers, account execs, clients and other mildly retarded mortals. Good creative people often have a better feel for the problem than the committee that wrote the strategy. When you are evaluating a campaign idea, it's not enough to say 'this is off strategy'. You must also ask yourself, 'is this a better strategy than the one we have?'

   If the answer is yes, you're going to have a lousy week. You have to go back and un-sell a strategy that has probably taken months to develop, has been up and down the client organization, and has lots of (often flawed) research to back it up. Somehow, you have to convince a whole bunch of people that all the work they've been doing for the past few months is wrong.

   Sound impossible? That's why you get the big bucks.

3. *Be eternally skeptical of grand strategic insights*

   Planners, researchers and their ilk love to take a little information and turn it into a heroic vision. Beware of this. Most valuable insights are small and contingent. There is almost nothing you can say about human behavior that is universal. Including this.

I was once at an advertising conference and a planning director was making a presentation. She was talking about groups she was conducting for a bank. The groups were going nowhere. She asked a participant "If you could invent the perfect bank, what would it be like?" He sat there for a minute or two without answering.

"I suddenly realized," she said, "I had the answer right there before me. People don't want to think about their bank. Then I knew I had the strategy: Bank of Whatever. It's the bank you don't have to think about."

I have a different explanation for the above. She asked a stupid question and the respondent sat there dazed and confused.

From the flimsiest of observations, she drew a grand, idiotic conclusion. And worst of all, the agency and the client bought it.

4. *Simplify and specify*
   I've seen thousands of ads that were too complicated or too generic. I've never seen one that was too simple or too specific.

5. *Remember why people buy stuff*
   There is an old blues song that goes like this:

   Feelin' good
   Feelin' good
   All the money in the world spent on
   *Feelin' good**

The guy who wrote that lyric understands marketing better than any Stanford MBA I've ever worked with. That's what commerce is about—people spending money to acquire things they think will make them feel good.

* by J. B. Lenoir, Jim Dickinson

Save your dark, pessimistic vision for your screenplay. Which reminds me . . .

6. *You're a salesman, not an artist*

Want to be an artist? God bless you. So do I. I wish us both good luck. But first you probably need to quit your day job. As a creative director, your job is to sell stuff. If you don't like that, I don't blame you. It's dirty work and hard on the creative ego.

If you are not comfortable being a salesman you will not be comfortable or successful being a creative director.

Does this mean it's impossible to create advertising that rises to the level of art? No. Every generation has a few people who can do that. But trust me on this one, it ain't you.

CLIENTS ASK ALL THE WRONG QUESTIONS

Any agency person who's ever participated in a new business pitch has been asked this question: "What is the process you use to develop advertising ideas?"

Any agency person with an ounce of integrity has answered this way: "Schmuck, there is no process."

In other words, no agency person has ever answered that way.

There may be a process for developing a strategy; there may be a process for developing a media plan; but there is no process for giving birth to an idea.

There never has been and there never will be.

Nonetheless, when asked the question, the agency usually trots out a chart with arrows and boxes and buckets and silos and feedback loops and checkpoints and all manner of obfuscatory baloney.

The chart usually has a very pompous sounding title, like "Developmental Matrix" and it shows how through consumer ethnographic analysis the idea starts as a small spark of insight and then by some highly evolved system it is inflated into a grand unifying concept.

In other words, it's a full 7-course bullshit banquet.

How it really happens is like this: a writer and art director are locked in a cage. A creative director opens the cage door just wide enough to throw in 5 pounds of briefing documents, memos, research reports, and old ads. He slams the door, yells "I need this shit by Thursday, and it better be fucking good" and runs off to lunch with his assistant.

How do you like the process now, amigo?

HOW APPLE DOES IT

Apple is not just the most successful consumer tech company on the planet, it is also the galaxy's most successful marketing company.

An article last week in *The Wall Street Journal* gives us some insight into how they have made their Apple stores into a retail juggernaut. More people visit Apple stores in a quarter than visit the four largest Disney amusement parks in a year.

Not surprisingly, how they have done it is by essentially ignoring all the "best practices" of business gurus and new age marketing nitwits.

While the oft-quoted gaggle of speakers who make the rounds of marketing conferences keep telling us we need to empower our employees and be transparent to our customers, Apple keeps its employees on a very short leash, essentially dictates the language they are allowed to use with customers, and fires anyone who thinks he or she ought to be having an "online conversation" about the company.

From the Wall Street Journal:

". . . A look at confidential training manuals, a recording of a store meeting and interviews with more than a dozen current and former employees reveal some of Apple's store secrets. They include: intensive control of how employees interact with customers, scripted training for on-site tech support . . . and anyone caught writing about the Cupertino, California, company on the Internet is fired . . ."

The astonishing part of all this is that to the advertising and marketing communities the lessons of Apple's amazing success are apparently invisible.

Here is a brief summary of Apple's consumer advertising activity as observed by this writer:

- Apple spends a ton of money on traditional advertising, in particular TV and outdoor.
- Apple's advertising looks much the same as it did 10 years

ago. Apple's advertising is always product focused. The product itself is usually smack dab in the middle of the page or screen. There is never any "lifestyle" or "branding" nonsense.

- From what I can see, Apple spends next to nothing on social media and almost all their online ad budget on something that actually works—search.

- Apple's "engagement" strategy with customers is not built around dopey online gimmicks but with well-controlled, tightly managed, face-to-face communication between people and customers.

- Apple fires those who engage in online "conversations" about the brand.

It would be hard to draw-up a set of behaviors that more thoroughly repudiate contemporary marketing dogma.

With all the success Apple has had, you'd think CMO's, agencies, and marketing "experts" would take a step back, take a look at what Apple has accomplished, and try to learn from it.

Instead they are mired in their own delusional feedback loop and blind to the evidence of their own eyes.

Chapter 3

Cranky Advice and Opinions

I WAS HOPING FOR A CENTERFOLD

AdPulp is one of the most popular of the advertising blogs. In April of 2009, David Burn, editor of AdPulp, interviewed me.

. . .

The *AdPulp* Interview: Bob Hoffman

Bob Hoffman is a funny guy in the tough as balls New York City tradition. He's also an insightful business leader running a 100+ person ad agency headquartered in San Francisco.

Hoffman's had the occasion to visit Portland recently—his daughter goes to school here—and this has led to some great face-to-face conversations over breakfast and again over coffee. This interview is an extension of those discussions.

Q. What led you to start Hoffman | Lewis?

A. Desperation.

I was in my early forties. After freelancing for three years I came to the realization that in the not-too-distant future I would be 50. I recognized that a 50-year-old freelancer was an old man but a 50-year-old CEO was a young man. I decided to be a young man.

Q. What led you to begin blogging? Will you continue writing the blog long term?

A. I started it almost two years ago out of frustration. I got sick of all the bullshit I was reading every day. After two weeks I said everything I wanted to say, but I've kept going because it's fun.

I won't continue it long term. It's too dangerous. I'm amazed a client hasn't fired me.

Q. You say no one's figured out how to make money with online content—including *The New York Times*—and that brands are wasting money in an area where there's "no formula," only experimentation. Please elaborate.

A. These are two different but related issues.

1. Artists' works used to be among the most highly valued of commodities and were protected by law. While technically they still are, the laws seem virtually unenforceable. This has already nearly ruined the music industry, and threatens the movie, television and newspaper industries.

Web maniacs applaud this as some fuzzy-headed form of democratization. They don't understand that democracy respects and protects personal property—including intellectual property. I don't think they'd be quite as sanguine about it if it were their paychecks being "democratized."

Online content is now expected to be free. AdPulp has several thousand readers a day. You're entitled to something for the news/entertainment/information you provide. I know how hard you work. You work all day, every day to provide it. But they expect it for free. Why? Do they work for free?

2. As for brands wasting money on line, it's like this. There have been a few big online advertising successes. But for every success there have been a thousand dismal flops. This is the dirty little secret that no one in marketing talks about.

Remember, advertising is a minor annoyance at best. Traditional advertising causes forced exposure—if you're going to watch American Idol you have to see my Coke spot whether you want to or not. Online advertising is different. You have to volunteer for it. The idea that people will voluntarily turn themselves in, or can be tricked, coaxed, or charmed into interacting with most brands, is a fantasy propagated by naivete and ideology.

Yes, there have been a few big successes. They seem random and ad hoc. They are mostly one-offs.

Q. What's the best thing about living in San Francisco? Is it a good city to conduct business?

A. San Francisco is a terrible city for business. Rents are high, taxes are high, salaries are high, living expenses are high, and most of the cab drivers are high.

The best thing about living here is that there are two baseball teams, good Mexican food, and a lot of bars.

Q. Would you pay to read any ad blogs? If so, which ones and why?

A. Advertising is a fairly interesting subject but most of the blog writing is dreary and predictable.

The only one I would pay to read is AdScam. Not because of the content, but because Parker is so funny.

Q. What's the most important thing you do as CEO of the agency?

A. Keep my partners from killing each other.

Q. What do you think of Lee Clow's media lab ideas? It seems he's trying to rebrand (and expand) the agency offering.

A. I have some ideas about where the ad business is going. They are very different from Lee's. If I were you, I'd bet on Lee.

Q. Will Hoffman | Lewis remain an indie shop?

A. Yes.

Q. Do you have a favorite TV show?

A. The only things I watch on TV are baseball, Seinfeld reruns, and documentaries about sea otters.

Q. Who do you most admire in business and why?

A. Steve Jobs. The best ad guy of this generation.

Q. What's the ad business going to look like in 20 years?

A. It will look like the Japanese ad industry. A few huge entities controlling everything.

All ads will be "rated" by a highly politicized "consumer review board" and will have to display their ratings.

The internet will be the punch line to jokes about stupid, primitive technology.

Seth Godin will still be writing that advertising is dead.

Talking animals will still not be funny.

Copywriters will be required to wear capes and Mouseketeer ears.

Q. What's your take on alternative compensation models? Should agencies and clients have a performance-based system in place?

A. Ideally, yes. The problem is it's impossible to isolate the effect of advertising from all the other variables. Consequently analyzing success, in any realm other than direct response, is very difficult.

Q. Are you only as good as your last ad?

A. I'm even worse.

MY NEW FACEBOOK STRATEGY

Half my Facebook friends I don't know. The other half I don't like. So I'm thinking about a new strategy for my Facebook page.

It started a few weeks ago when I decided to cull my 'friends.'

First I unfriended everyone who was using Facebook as a Twitter substitute. (Here's a tip. Nobody gives a damn that it's sunny in your backyard, okay?)

Then I unfriended everyone who used Facebook to bore the hell out of me with their stupid political opinions.

Then I unfriended everyone guilty of gratuitous over-sharing. (Another tip: Your personal hygiene, sex, and bowel habits are best kept to yourself.)

Then I unfriended everyone who thought Facebook was a scrap-book for posting every picture they had of their rotten brats.

Then I unfriended everyone who flaunted their important big-shot friends.

I'm now down to about 75 friends and it feels really good. It's like cleaning all that ugly old crap out of your closet.

So here's my new strategy. I'm thinking of taking it to the next level. I'm thinking that I'll set a limit of 50 friends.

I'll give a free pass to my daughter, my real friends, and the other 3 or 4 people I actually like. The rest have to earn their way on.

They either have to post entertaining updates, or take me out for pizza (thin crust, no f***ing pineapple) or do something to earn their way on. Maybe I'll charge $1,000.

Then I'll rank them.

Every few weeks I'll drop #50 and give someone new a chance. If they perform they can stay. If I find out they're branding consultants, or don't drink, or think Whoopi Goldberg is funny, they're gone.

By the way, no credit cards. Cash or check only.

REALITY AT THE DMV

Last week I had the good fortune to spend an hour renewing my driver's license.

Most people would consider a trip to the DMV about as appealing as listening to a 50-slide powerpoint presentation about search engine optimization. But I'm thinking of making a monthly visit to the DMV a condition of employment for everyone on my staff.

I want them to see what the people they're making ads for really look like. I want them to see the people they never see at the restaurants they go to; never see at the bars they frequent; never see at the focus groups they attend; and never hear from on Twitter.

In other words, I want them to see the "consumer" they're all so very certain they know everything about.

As the CEO of a substantial media company said in an email to me recently:

"There is a huge problem in America where the people making decisions, who grew up in comfortable homes, went to expensive colleges and landed relatively plush jobs, think that the Average American is just like them. It just isn't true but this mindset frames enormous decisions in many industries including media."

So, please, do yourself a favor. Go to your nearest non-leafy DMV and spend an hour. And see if you come away still thinking that America is online having "conversations about brands."

YET ANOTHER CRANK THEORY

If you've been alive more than 45 minutes you've probably noticed something—people do really stupid things.

I don't mean stupid like misspelling February. I mean stupid like shooting meth, or piercing their eyelids, or watching *Entertainment Tonight*. The kind of stupid that can kill you or turn you into a zombie.

If you look deeply enough into any one person's life, I'm pretty sure you can find something stupidly destructive in it.

The question is, why?

I guess Freud would say it has something to do with penises or the absence thereof.

But I have a different opinion.

I think it's about boredom.

I think people will do anything to avoid boredom—they'll jump out of airplanes, they'll wrestle alligators, they'll go to social media conferences.

It doesn't matter how stupid it is, if it relieves or impedes boredom, people will do it.

It's the only explanation I can come up with for line dancing, rock climbing and Facebook.

But I'll finish this later. Right now, I'm bored.

THE FUTURE IS BEHIND US

Memo To Staff:

For several years now, we have been known as the agency of the future. How can we claim this? Because it says so right on our website!

It has not been easy being the agency of the future. But thanks to our commitment to empowering our empowerment, and tearing down walls, and breaking down silos, and updating our Facebook page, and Content Technology, Search, CMS, WCM, MRX, ECM, Multilingual, E20, KM, and XML we are at the forefront of agencies whose websites say they are the agency of the future!

Of this we can be proud.

But the world is changing rapidly. Today the consumer is in charge. In the past, nobody knew who was in charge. Sometimes people with nice suits were in charge. Sometimes it seemed like Wolf Blitzer was in charge. Then there was the time when the Spice Girls were in charge.

But now we know who's in charge, and it's the consumer. Just send out a tweet asking, "Who's in charge?" You'll soon get back plenty of replies telling you that it's the consumer. (Ignore the tweets from my cousin Sheldon who thinks he's in charge. He's not.)

We are living through a very tumultuous era. It is time for us to realize that the future is behind us.

We can no longer be satisfied being the agency of the future. Today, we have to look beyond the future, to a time when the future will be but a distant memory.

We must realize that in today's inter-globally connected world, inter-connectivity is globular. And maybe not just globular, but inter-globular! Our clients expect that our inter-globularity will exceed their expectations and create the opportunity for a multi-channel globuverse.

Those who do not respond to the changes that are happening all around us will be left behind to do radio spots and pay for their own football tickets.

Recently, your management team had its annual retreat. The theme was *Preparing For The New Future By Being Prepared And Looking Forwarder, 3000.*

We tackled this thorny subject head-on. We spent three no-holds-barred days discussing the branding of our brand in light of the new realities of the digital revolution and all that mobile stuff. We had Powerpoint presentations, and "conversations," and everything.

After one particularly penetrating session, a deep insight was revealed.

We have to realize that it is not enough to execute sound strategies. We have to have a strategy for our strategies—how will our strategies be strategically different from the strategies of our competitors?

In other words, we need a strategy strategy.

To accomplish this, I have appointed a team from our executive committee. They will be known as "The Team From Our Executive Committee." Their first job will be to find a consulting firm to help us develop our strategy strategy.

In order to accomplish this as rapidly as possible, we have hired a consultant to help us identify the consulting firm that will help us develop our strategy strategy.

I am very excited to be part of an exciting effort to leave the old future behind and develop a new future for us all. We can all do our part by *Preparing For The New Future By Being Prepared And Looking Forwarder!*

NOTHING HUMAN WORKS AS ADVERTISED

I'm astonished when people are surprised at the failures of capitalism, or socialism, or communism.

I'm amazed when people are stunned that Democratic policies don't work. Or Republican policies. Or liberal policies, or conservative policies.

I'm astounded when people express dismay that Wall Street is stupid, or government is wasteful.

I laugh when I hear people complain that economists were wrong, or that an education scheme didn't pan out, or that a social policy had the opposite of its intended effect.

How much history do you have to read until you realize that there is no right way to do things, just different wrong ways? How many failures does it take to realize that systems devised by humans never work as advertised?

The longer a system survives, the more obvious its flaws become. It's like the slight wobble of a top. The longer it spins the worse it gets.

The best we can do is to identify the systems that wobble the least.

YOU CAN'T STOP THE GRAPH

"Ad Contrarian," people often say to me, "how come you're always so relaxed and nonchalant while the rest of us are so aggravated?"

I say, "Sit down my friend and let's talk." Then I light my pipe, kick off my slippers, and sit back in my rocker.

"We humans have been around this sorry planet for about 200,000 years. The planet has been around for 4.5 billion years. So what portion of the Earth's life have we been part of? The answer is .00004. This is not a large number ."

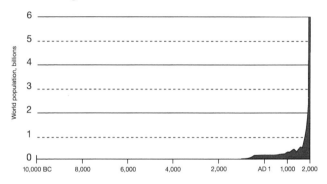

Then I take out the graph you see above. "You see this graph above?" I say. "This shows human population over the past 12,000 years. For most of that time, we were just a minor annoyance. But a couple of hundred years ago we started multiplying like, um, humans. And we became an epidemic.

"There is no way in hell or, more to the point, on Earth, that this growth is sustainable. None.

"Just for a moment, I want you to forget all the nonsense that politicians and poets and holy men and newspapers fill you full of, and take another look at the graph. No graph of anything ever in history was able to continue up a straight line. It just doesn't work that way. And this one won't either. Which means catastrophe is coming. It may be environmental, or cosmic, or nuclear, or medical. I have no idea. It may be quick or it may be long and drawn out. Who knows? It may be tomorrow or a thousand years from tomorrow. Can't tell. But the graph says it's coming, and I never argue with graphs.

"So, why am I nonchalant? Sure I want the A's to win the American League West, but I'm not going to get too aggravated if they don't. Yes, I wouldn't mind getting the Nobel Prize, or the Coke account, but I'm not going to get all pissy if they don't come through. And if my candidate doesn't win the presidency . . . well, do you really think he can stop the graph?

"Oh, and while you're up, would you mind passing that bottle?"

ADVERTISING AND THE FUTURE OF APPLE

After Steve Jobs stepped down as CEO of Apple last week, speculation about the company's future began immediately.

The consensus seemed to be that Jobs built a strong culture, hired smart people, and taught a way of thinking that will serve Apple well in the future. The story line went like this—while Jobs will be missed, he is no longer essential to the future of the company and it will go on brilliantly without him.

I don't buy this for a second. Genius is non-transferable.

Jobs hasn't just created better computers, he has created a world that nobody else could envision. He brought an artist's sensibility to a field previously populated by capable but tone-deaf engineers. He didn't just make beautiful looking hardware, he took what was a dead screen full of little green letters on a blue background and turned it into an astounding, enchanting world of graphics, music, and video that has become a central feature of contemporary life.

He has made work more fun, knowledge more available, and entertainment more rewarding.

Anyone who has had the pleasure of buying an Apple product knows the great aesthetic delight of turning it on for the first time and seeing the beauty that ensues. Even going to an Apple store is a completely unique and strangely arresting experience.

On Friday, Apple became the world's largest company, surpassing ExxonMobil in market value. It will not simply evaporate. The most likely scenario is that Apple will continue to shine for several years while the initiatives that Jobs started are still in the pipeline, and then slowly the company's radiance will start to dim. They will be successful and will continue to produce excellent products for a long time— but the startling brilliance will slowly fade.

Many successful creative enterprises turn out to be the extended shadow of one individual. My best guess is that Apple is such an enterprise.

Interestingly, one of the first indications of whether Apple is capable of continuing its explosion of creative energy without Jobs at the helm may be found in its advertising. The product pipeline will take years to screw up. But the ad pipeline can be screwed up in no time.

About a year from now, with Jobs in the background, the knuckleheads at Apple (there are knuckleheads everywhere) will have a chance to get their sweaty hands on the advertising.

Jobs is a brilliant technology visionary. But let's not forget that he is also the best ad man of his generation. He is what you might call a "classicist." Apple advertising is simple. It is almost always product-focused (the product usually sits smack dab in the middle of a white page.) The TV spots for the iPad and iPhone are usually nothing more than simple but compelling product demonstrations.

Here are some clues to look for in Apple's advertising that will indicate that dull hands are grabbing at the wheel:

1. *Creeping Brandism:* The Apple brand was built bottom-up. That is, the products defined the brand. Virtually every Apple ad was about a product, not the brand (okay, there was "Think Different" but that didn't last.) Keep an eye out for the erosion of this discipline.

2. *Agency change:* Vapid marketing people relegated to the background all these years by Jobs' dominance may suddenly start flexing. They wouldn't dare contradict Jobs' legacy, but they could accomplish the same thing by undermining the agency.

3. *The Tortured Logic of Account Planning:* Look for ads about you the consumer instead of Apple products. Look for moronic online "engagement" gimmicks. Or look for social media pandering.

4. *Complications:* Part of the brilliance of Apple advertising has been its simplicity. Keep an eye out for complicated ideas or ads with more than one product.

5. *Media:* Apple has used online media sparingly. The preponderance of its advertising has been conducted in traditional media—TV, print, and outdoor. Watch to see if Apple suddenly starts going all trendy and new age in its media choices.

If you start seeing any of these signs coming out of Cupertino, sell your shares.

Advertising will be an early indicator of whether people without vision and taste are moving in at Apple. It will be interesting to watch.

BIG DUMB GLOBAL GUESTS

Every now and then some big, global agency comes sniffing around trying to buy us. Usually it's because their agency in San Francisco is a disaster, or they want to get their hands on one of our accounts.

Recently it was driven home to me why we've never taken any of these guys seriously. The ceo of a very large agency came around. He's sitting in our conference room. He leans across the conference table. The first question he asks is, *"So, Bob, what would you say are your core competencies?"*

What are our core competencies? What are our core competencies? We're an AD AGENCY. What do you THINK our core competencies are? Folk dancing? Knitting? Cheese making? We make ADS, schmuck. That's our core competency!

No, I didn't say that. My mother taught me to be nice to guests. Even big, dumb, global guests.

SIMPLIFIERS AND COMPLICATORS

About a thousand years ago I wrote a piece for *Adweek* called "Simplifiers and Complicators". It was so long ago, *Adweek* wasn't even called *Adweek*.

Every now and then I run into someone who reminds me of the piece. It happened again last week.

I can't remember the specifics of the article, but the point was that there are two kinds of people: people who simplify things and people who complicate them. In most businesses, complicators are annoying. In advertising they are ruinous.

Every time you create an ad there are a million things to say about the brand or product. The key to producing a successful ad is in understanding what is essential and what is extraneous. Simplifiers have the ability to cut down the weeds and clear a path. Complicators cannot distinguish between the pertinent and the irrelevant.

If you're working with an account exec or a creative director who is a complicator, you understand the frustration involved. If you're working with a client who's a complicator, you're probably thinking about that fry job at Burger King.

In an ad agency, one highly placed complicator can undo the good work of a dozen simplifiers.

Chapter 4

The Digital Dream World

DIGITAL DREAM WORLD

Welcome to the new world.

It's a world in which people are eager to interact with ads. It's a world in which consumers want to have relationships with brands and conversations with marketers. It's a world that is causing a revolution in advertising and marketing.

Unfortunately, it's a world that exists largely in our dreams.

Let's start with a little background. Have you noticed that what was once called "interactive advertising" is now referred to as "display advertising?" The term "interactive" has been quietly bundled off to its room and told to be quiet.

Advertising interactivity was the first of our pleasant little digital dreams. In this dream, people would be more engaged and interact with our ads, making the ads far more effective. The logic went like this: "Um . . . people like to interact with the medium, so, um, ya know, they'll like to, ya know, interact with the ads, too." The only problem is, people don't want to interact with ads. Bastards.

Click-through rates are now hovering below one-tenth of 1 percent. That means 99.9 percent of the time people aren't even engaged enough to move a finger. Naive clients, however, bought the fantasy of advertising interactivity lock, stock and pixel.

Slowly and quietly "interactivity" as a rationale for online display advertising was retired before it became too much of an embarrassment. These days, the sales pitch for online advertising sounds remarkably like the sales pitch for traditional print advertising.

But don't worry. We have a new dream world. It's a world in which consumers want to have relationships with brands and socialize with marketers online, and have conversations with us. It's being fueled by the sensational rise in popularity of social media. However, I'm afraid this dream will turn out to be every bit as misguided as the last one.

When social media experts start talking, I get the same feeling I get when listening to political debates. My eyes glaze over, my jargon detector jumps into the red zone and I get an urge to dive through plate glass.

Pitches for social media marketing almost always start with a recitation of startling facts about social media—how Facebook has more members than there are grains of sand in the universe, how the average American spends over 28 hours per day with social media. You've heard the pitch.

What they don't seem to understand is that there's a difference between social media and social media *marketing*. The fact that social media has experienced phenomenal popularity is not prima facie evidence of the magical powers of social media marketing.

The new logic goes like this: "Um . . . people like to interact with each other so, um, ya know, they'll like to, ya know, interact with us, too."

From what I can tell, there are two things consumers are enthusiastic about when it comes to online social behavior: Connecting with each other and getting something for nothing from us.

I can't prove it, but I'll bet you $10 that the primary reason people become "friends" or "followers" of brands on Facebook and Twitter is not to have a conversation with the marketer, but to get a discount, a special offer, a deal, or some other form of insider information or advantage. It's the same reason they join a frequent flier plan. They don't want a relationship with a baggage handler; they want a free flight to Hawaii.

Yes, I know there are examples of brands that have been successful with "conversational" social media strategies. We always hear about them. We never hear about the thousands of failures.

Yes, I also know there are people who are unaccountably fond of a particular brand of mayonnaise and want to have a conversation with the marketer about it. But let's be honest here. Those people are weird.

Most days, your sensible consumer doesn't have the time, patience, or inclination to have a conversation with her husband. Why in the world would she want to have a conversation with us?

Having a social media marketing strategy is a good thing. But if your strategy is contingent on the idea that consumers want to have a conversation with you, create a relationship with your company and engage with your brand, you may be living in a dream world.

If you want to avoid the digital dream world, build your strategy on a foundation of reality. Give people an interesting way to connect with each other, and then give them something for nothing.

It's not all that complicated. But just like the last time around, the lesson the ad industry is resolutely committed to not learning is that in the digital world people are passionate about interacting with each other. Not ads. Not brands. Not you. Not me.

GRAVITY AND THE WEB

Driving through Berkeley, near where I live, it's not unusual to see a beat-up, old VW bus with a bumper sticker that reads, "Think Globally, Act Locally."

Unfortunately, if there's one thing we humans are not very good at, it's thinking globally. We have an unfortunate tendency to think very locally. I see it every July in San Francisco—people from New Jersey, dressed in T-shirts and shorts, freezing their asses off because they think summer here is like summer there.

A wonderful example occurred after Richard Nixon won a 49-state landslide victory in 1972. Pauline Kael, then film critic for *The New Yorker*, famously said, "How can that be? I don't know a single person who voted for Nixon." (By the way, that quote has been attributed to about 1,000 other people.)

Alan Wolk calls it "Nascar blindness." Our inability to understand the behavior of those outside our feedback loop.

Which brings me to gravity. Gravity is everywhere. Consequently, we think of gravity as a very powerful force that keeps us glued to the ground and brings huge airplanes crashing down around us. Actually, science tells us that gravity is a very weak force. In fact, it's the weakest known force in the universe.

To prove this, go to a children's toy store and buy one of those little 50-cent horseshoe magnets. Then put a paper clip on the ground. Place the magnet above the paper clip. You now have two competing forces—the electro-magnetic force of the little magnet pulling up on the paper clip versus the gravitational force of the entire Earth pulling down on the paper clip. The little magnet wins.

The electro-magnetic force is actually 1,000,000,000,000,000,000, 000,000,000,000,000,000 times stronger than gravity. But because gravity is all around us, we mistakenly think of it as uniquely powerful.

The same is true of the Web. Most advertising and marketing people have come to believe that because the Internet is so pervasive in our lives it must be a strong advertising force. So far it has not been. While the Web itself has become massively influential, advertising on the Web has proven to be problematic and, in many cases, dismayingly ineffectual.

Of course, Internet advertising is a lot of different things. It's display ads, search, e-mail, viral and paid videos, social media, podcasts, blogs, widgets, apps. It's a grab bag of dissimilar stuff that for the sake of simplicity we have come to refer to as "online advertising." It's unfair to say that all of it is ineffectual.

So far, there has been one type of online advertising that has been a clear and unqualified success: search. But search is limited. Mostly, we use search once we have already decided to buy, much like we used the Yellow Pages. Search fulfills demand; it doesn't create demand.

The ultimate test for the power of an advertising medium is its ability to contribute in a critical way to the building of a brand. In its 13 years or so as a mainstream medium, the Web has not proven to me that it's capable of building consumer-facing, non-Web-native brands.

Thirteen years into the mainstream life of TV, it had become an enormously powerful advertising medium and had been instrumental in creating scores of robust consumer-facing brands in dozens of categories.

Can anyone name even five serious non-native, consumer-facing brands that have been built primarily by Web advertising? Is there a major brand of coffee, butter, beer, bread, chicken, gasoline, soda, peanut butter, dog food, milk, tires, potato chips, life insurance, lawn mowers, toothbrushes—you get the point—that has been built primarily by Web advertising? I'm a little slow, but frankly, I can't even think of one.

Yes, the Web has been effective at building Web-native brands like Google, Zappos, Amazon and Facebook. It's as if the only brands TV was good at creating were CBS, NBC, ABC and Comcast

The facts about online advertising continue to be discouraging:

1. Click-through rates on display ads have dropped abysmally and currently are about one in a thousand.

2. According to Nielsen, 98 percent of all video is still watched on that old dinosaur, the TV.

3. As for advertising on social media, it's probably unfair to judge the value of Facebook advertising solely on click-through-rates since it's sold mainly on a cost-per-click basis. Nonetheless, it's a bit alarming that typical click-through rates on Facebook ads hover at about 2 in 10,000. (Adweek magazine reported the number as 5 in 10,000 last week. My number comes from a Facebook insider.)

Of course, digital advertising zealots are as fervent as ever. The continued growth of online spending indicates that it is still possible to torture the data in such a way as to make a convincing case for online advertising.

But I'm starting to get a sense that the "irrational exuberance" marketers have shown for Web advertising, while still naively out of proportion to its effectiveness, is beginning to show signs of coming into alignment with reality.

It is quite possible that the marketing and advertising industries are starting to believe what a lot of us have been thinking for a long time. Like gravity, Internet advertising is all around us. And also like gravity, it is a less powerful force than it appears to be.

OH, NO. I'M DEAD!

For the past four years, one of the mainstays of this blog has been making fun of the silly "_____ Is Dead" brand of marketing journalism.

If you'd like to see your name on the byline of a magazine article, but you have no idea what to write about, just pick any topic—let's say "shopping"—and write an article called *"Shopping Is Dead."*

The great thing is, you don't need any facts. You just make up a few assertions based on nothing but the latest industry hooey, and they publish it. It's great!

We've been through "Advertising is Dead" and "Television is Dead" and just about everything else associated with Life Before The Internet (LBTI) has been declared dead, too.

The fact that things go on pretty much as before is irrelevant to the minds that produce and believe this nonsense. So what if television viewing is at its highest point ever? So what if the world is drowning in advertising as never before? Web maniacs want them dead so, what the hell, let's just say they're dead.

The reason that facts have no place in this type of journalism is that these pieces aren't really about what they claim to be about. They are not about advertising or television. They are about a particular brand of religion—*The Divine Church Of The Internet* —and these paeans are part of an evolving liturgy written in adoration of the new god. Sadly, he's a jealous god who cannot be satisfied unless he vanquishes everything that came before him.

In this new religion we don't just have a new god, we also have a New Man. The New Man has shed the wickedness of his previously pagan existence and is now cleansed and enlightened by the shining light of the Internet.

Today we present a lovely example of the genre. It's called *The Copywriter Is Dead.* It appeared last week in a blog called *The Future Of Media.* According to this latest addition to the *Encyclopedia Of Things That Are Dead,* we copywriters have "perfected the art of lying to consumers" and for that and our other sins we have now been exiled to the boneyard.

Can you guess what killed us? Hint: It not only killed us, it also changed everything. Ah, you clever boy, you've got it. We were killed by social media.

The article gives us a full curriculum on the amazing blessings of social media, including all the usual stuff—"cultural curation", "lines of conversation","avenues of authenticity." Strangely, however, nothing about congressmen tweeting pictures of their weenies.

Apparently, the reason for the tragic demise of us poor copywriters is that now in the age of social media...

"... *the voice of the real individual has triumphed—only the recommendation of a like-minded consumer, journalist or objective reviewer holds sway.*"

Really? That's a pretty sweeping statement. So I decided to do a little research and find out in what proportion these "like-minded consumers, journalists, and objective reviewers" are responsible for my untimely demise.

I parked myself in front of the Safeway in my neighborhood with a clipboard and pencil. As people came out with their shopping carts, I stopped them, picked one or two items out of their basket and asked them this question: "Who did you consult before you bought this jar of peanut butter and those frozen chicken fingers: a like-minded consumer, a journalist, or an objective reviewer?"

Here are the tabulated responses:

- Like-minded consumer: 0
- Journalist: 0
- Objective Reviewer: 0
- Nobody: 585
- Get The Hell Out of Here: 1,207

Although these numbers tend not to support the author's hypothesis, being a fair-minded person I must admit that my local Safeway is probably a little down-market compared to the author of the piece, whose credentials include producing "experiential" work for "global brands." I imagine in those rarefied quarters where global brands are experientiated you probably can't swing a dead yoga mat without hitting a card-carrying cultural curator.

As a result of my research project, I have come to the conclusion that what consumers rely on mostly is their own freakin' experience. Can it be that the personal experience of enjoying a product is even more powerful than the triumphant voices of all the twittering "like-minded consumers, journalists, and objective reviewers?" Can it be that we're not all slaves to what others "like?"

And that's where copywriters come in.

The job of the copywriter is to persuade us to experience a product. It's a job that requires a good deal of artistry, finesse, and tact—characteristics rarely encountered in the silly jabber of web zealots.

PUDDING HEADS

DOTAC (Daughter of *The Ad Contrarian*) sent me a link today. Apparently some geniuses called *Pudding Media* are going to provide you with free VOIP phone service if you will let them listen in on your calls and send you ads that relate to your conversations.

Of course, this will not intrude on your privacy. "Mr. Maislos (chief executive) said that Pudding Media had considered the privacy question carefully. The company is not keeping recordings or logs of the content of any phone calls . . ." Yeah, right. Anyone want to bet this ends up in a huge "oh, we're so sorry we overstepped our bounds" scandal?

TAC predicts: Within a few years congress will haul all these clowns (including Google, which monitors your email subjects) up to Capitol Hill and rip them a new one.

And nothing will happen.

People are willing to give up privacy for convenience.

Kudos to DOTAC, only a high school kid, who understands the dangers in this a lot better than the new media hustlers do.

SOCIAL MEDIA MADNESS GOES GLOBAL

Just when you think that utopian social media claptrap has about run its course, along comes something that renews your faith in the ability of web-addled maniacs to create infinite permutations of infantile nonsense.

And lest you think that America has a monopoly on social media madness, this thing comes our way via a recent article in *B&T* in Australia. According to the piece . . .

"We are now living our lives in a perpetual state of beta through social media."

Ohmygod, a perpetual state of beta! And I thought it was just a little case of irritable bowel syndrome . . .

". . . it's a place where opportunity and innovation exist interdependently presenting us with new paths and a new narrative; stories that inspire a sense of belonging to something bigger than ourselves. Understanding this fully is, in part, learning how we can authentically drive content across platforms to create new experiences."

Wow. Who knew? I imagined I was just posting some stuff on Facebook about how my friend's cat peed on his new golf bag. Turns out I'm authentically driving content across platforms to create new experiences! You gotta admit, I'm pretty awesome.

"Ultimately, it's about learning how we can transform from being content producers to 'context producers' as we reflect reconnection in our products, culture, and people."

Well that settles it. I am so going to reflect reconnection in my products, culture and people. Apparently, social media is . . .

". . . a frontier where creative and strategic partnerships play out in a heroic celebration of the everyday, and which are bound together by a new currency that considers peoples' lives . . . This is more than an altruistic pipe dream—it's the emergent context made possible by sociological technical advancement."

So here's a question. Do you have to be completely demented to be a social media director? Because this guy is clearly wicked nuts.

An "heroic celebration of the everyday?" In social media? Is this guy crazy? Social media is morons like me posting pictures of our dogs sleeping.

"The sheer profundity of our ability to bring together people of diverse background, geography, passion, interest and opinion, to create dynamic value and competitive advantage is evidence of what the future holds."

Dude, calm down. Here's what the future holds—the same crap as now, only worse.

A BLOG IS LIKE A HUSBAND

There are days when this blog takes over my life. Sometimes it is like having a husband:

- It needs constant attention and feeding
- If you don't prod it, it will just sit there and do nothing
- After a while you'll wonder why you ever thought it was exciting
- All your friends will think it's stupid
- It smells up the bathroom

Before you start a blog, take a close look at the worst husband you know.

Do you really want one of those?

SOCIAL MEDIA MARKETING ECOSYSTEM EXPLAINED

Here at *The Ad Contrarian* World Headquarters, there's nothing we like better than a good ecosystem.

So when we came across this awesome ecosystem for social media marketing, well, how do you resist it?

We know some of you Luddites just aren't up-to-date on these things. So, as a service to our readers, we are publishing the attached chart of the social media marketing ecosystem which we hijacked from a social media website.

Give it a good once over, and then a comprehensive explanation follows.

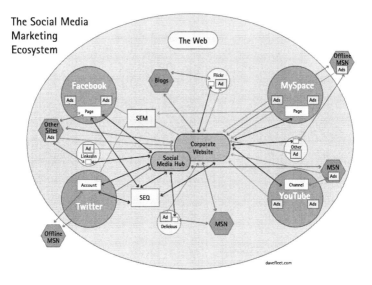

As you can see, the World Wide Web has four big shaded circles and some small ones. There are also boxes that resemble credit cards and things shaped like stop signs. The whole thing kind of looks like the nucleus of an atom designed by Congress. On the inside of all these shapes there are words that make social media geeks go vaporous, like "Twitter" and "YouTube." On the outside there are arrows.

The arrows go back and forth and crisscross and if they were made of wool they'd make a nice sweater. Sadly, two of MSN's stop signs have been ejected from the nucleus, but please don't tell Bill Gates about this or we'll all be in deep shit.

Okay, so I don't want to hear anymore of this crap that I don't understand social media.

SURE TO FAIL

According to *The New York Times,* diving into the pool of idiotic on-line ideas this week is Coors Light. They are launching a "Code Blue" app on Facebook.

"We talk a lot internally about '360-ing' our innovations," said Andy England, chief marketing officer at Coors Brewing . . .

Wow. 360-ing the innovations.

And what exactly is this innovation? It's the label that turns blue when it's cold because you really have to be a freaking genius to figure out when a bottle of beer is cold. Who said America lacks innovative ideas?

"Imagine being able to 'Code blue' someone on your iPhone," he (the group creative director . . . of Avenue A/Razorfish) added, "and say, 'I just got laid off; you better go buy me a Coors Light at the local bar.'"

Wow. Imagine. On my iPhone! How cool would that be!

Excuse me while I "86" this innovation.

CURRENCY ACROSS THE ECOSYSTEM

Stop the presses.

The Interactive Advertising Bureau, the Association of National Advertisers, and the American Association of Advertising Agencies, along with Bain & Company and MediaLink are banding together in the hope of "Making Measurement Make Sense."

This should be good for a few laughs.

Apparently, what this fuster-cluck is all about is finding a way to take all the incomprehensible, misleading, intentionally obfuscatory "data" that the online metrics geniuses are generating and getting something intelligible out of them. Good luck.

Making measurement make sense? These people can't even make their press releases make sense. According to a spokesman . . .

"Online media has an abundance of metrics, but none that serve as currency across the ecosystem."

Yeah, that's what we need—currency across the freakin' ecosystem.

I guess there's some solace to be taken in that these people are finally admitting what *Ad Contras* have been screaming about for years—that most online measurement is crapola masquerading as information.

This effort is doomed to failure. The enormous success of digital advertising is based on the fortunate circumstance that almost no one understands anything about the numbers. And those who do ain't talkin'.

Do you really think the ad industry wants to butcher the cash cow by clearly explaining how alarmingly unimpressive most of the metrics for digital advertising are?

These guys better make sure they don't do their job too well. If they suddenly forget their "currencies" and their "ecosystems" and start talking in plain English, we're all screwed.

CONVERSATION WITH A WEB MANIAC

This past weekend I had a web conversation with a guy named Felix who runs a digital ad company in the UK. The conversation was conducted via comments on a blog post of mine entitled "The Thing That Will Change Everything." Dave Trott, one of the UK's most respected admen, sent Felix over to the blog to read the post knowing Felix would disapprove. Here's the conversation between Felix and me.

Felix to The Ad Contrarian:

TAC . . . I'm sure you've got a trillion years of understanding consumer behaviour, and I'm sure you're right about how venal, faddish and self-important the marketers you work with are.

But here's the thing. The internet did change everything, utterly and without mercy. We have a globally distributed notion of justice. We have a globally distributed set of cultural norms. We (finally) have a near-universal language. We have a US President accepted as a good replacement for the universally reviled previous global leader who everyone in the world knows intimately, and who has been elected based on a third of the world's cultural norms. We have a world of consumers who elect and buy, taken over from a locale of consumers you used to sell to.

Consumer behaviour may not have changed. But expectation, motivation, influence and conversion to buy have changed forever. The consumer, finally, is king. And TV, though still a powerful medium, hasn't caught up despite 12 years of interactive TV. The day TV advertising can be segmented not by programme but by the individual consumer's implicit or explicit at-that-moment requirements will be the day TV gets back on its feet. And yes, when we started an interactive TV agency for Lowe in 1998 it was arguably way too early. The fact it produced interactive TV ads for Tesco and Unilver, two of the most far-sighted marketers, doesn't take away from the fact that it couldn't make money—but it was necessary to help get the ball that may one day save the TV advertising industry's arse rolling.

My own view about what people might remember is that it takes two types of people for progress to happen—the innovators and visionaries who come at things too early but set up the parameters of the experiment, and the reactionaries that temper the enthusiasm but enforce rigour. I'm quite happy to be in one of the groups, and I'm glad of the existence of the other, because your maturity means I can borrow, say, the discipline of data planning and prove that what we do works better for the new world's consumers than what you used to do when it was the only way.

Glad this social media thing is here though, because previously the only way we could have an argument was down the pub or in the letters pages, so thanks Twitterverse and blogosphere, at least you've revolutionised how fast one man can flourish his own reactionary views, another can highlight them, a third can get it all wrong before correcting his mistake, and how fast presumably this will turn into pixels in the wind. Personally I'd much prefer to do this over a pint than in public, but hey, you know that when even the Iranians are using Twitter to complain about injustice, the world's all gone and changed while you were busy watching television ;)

The Ad Contrarian to Felix:

To be honest, I would normally ignore your "visionary" comments as just the usual ravings of an online maniac.

But since Dave Trott sent you over here, and I admire Dave greatly, I'm going to take what you have to say seriously.

Extraordinary claims ("the internet did change everything, utterly") require extraordinary proof. You are very good at making the extraordinary claims, but a little weak on the evidence. Ten pounds of assertions do not equal one ounce of validation.

Let's take it point by point. First, we do not have a "globally distributed" notion of ANYTHING. The internet notwithstanding, there is just as much diversity of opinion about justice, and cultural norms and everything else political and cultural as there has ever been. Maybe you and your pals who read each others' blogs and tweets have reached a consensus, but the world is just as messy and full of conflict and discord as it has ever been. I would like to suggest that you try reading one of those old-fashioned things we "reactionaries" call a newspaper.

In the next paragraph you got one thing right: consumer behavior has not changed. Everything else in that paragraph is wrong. All that baloney about "expectation, motivation . . .", do you just make that shit up? Do your clients believe it? Here are some facts: 1) People now watch more TV than ever before. 2) Every test ever done on interactive TV has been a failure.

You are obviously an intelligent person. When you make assertions like "the internet did change everything" there are only two possibilities: either you mean what you say, or you are playing with words. If you are just playing with words, it's not worth commenting on. If you mean what you say, it is very disturbing.

There is a lot to life beyond the computer screen. There is food and music and art and friendship and talking and laughing and flowers and sports and, as you say, an argument down at the pub. To say that the internet changed everything is simply an alarming assertion for an intelligent person to make. You are spending way too much time in front of a computer screen.

PS: Just because I'm right, doesn't make me a "reactionary." Just because you're wrong, doesn't make you a "visionary."

Felix to The Ad Contrarian:

So this is me. I fly gliders, ride horses, have friends all over the world, throw parties, eat at nice restaurants, drive sports cars, same stuff as he. I have a reasonable online life as well, though very little outside of work hours. I keep in touch with the 200 or so people of every social, religious and political hue that I cherish in my personal life, and the 200 or so I value in my professional life, using my social media. But I'm no geek, I went to a school with no computers—unlike the current generation in the West and the new generation in the East that relies on bandwidth like air.

I was lucky to have been involved in starting one of the world's first web agencies, one of the first SEO agencies, the first iTV agency, and one of the leading eCRM agencies. I'm still learning all the time because our world is constantly changing, and still very often wrong (there, an easy one for you to quote me on later).

But the world has indeed changed. You've commented yourself on Tehran's new Twittering classes. That's a fine example of real-time, unfiltered interactive news, something that could not have happened before the net. In fact, where there remains no bandwidth TV still rules; but those are the same places where they launch missiles to mock independence day or misguided foreigners swim to meet housebound leaders. Iran's real-time-shared protestations are not iconic like Tianenmen Square, but then what's an icon but a fixation on the object and not the consumer of it. The new world has changed. This world is one where what a brand is is defined by what it lets its consumers say about it - not what it tells its consumers to think about it. And if you can't tell the difference between the two, then that's symptomatic of why the advertising industry has had its day in the sun.

You come from a world where the marketer defined the brand, and substantiated it with product. The world we now live in is one in which consumers commune, and brands that listen are defined by their listening, and their products get defined by what its consumers say—or show—they want un-prompted. This is how Unilever and Dell and P&G now work. On their rapid way out, thank goodness, are the days of the guided focus group, where ad folk with middling geography degrees divine market desires from "representative" samples of ten.

Advertising was first undermined by Direct Marketing, when the three letter lie in econometrics was exposed, and finally replaced with statistical certainty and relevance, something that TV panders but does not provide. Interactive TV was born of advertising people desperate to cling onto a world they could no longer control - of course it hasn't worked, except in hotels—where it's interactive but ad-free—and in the UK, where it forms the backbone to Domino Pizza's revenue stream and where finally the BBC has learned to serve multiple options to millions of viewers in news, Glastonbury (where your Boss played last weekend) and travel sales. Perhaps after all there too you're wrong.

Customers in their collective can make the decisions now, because brands that understand the way the world has changed listen to them, build their new products around them, and acquire brand equity by association. The brand onion is now more of a soup, a broth at best. 150 years ago you too changed the world. But today we know exactly which fifty percent does what, why, how and when.

TV may indeed be watched by more people, but there are also more cars, more polluters, more superpowers - and yet they are the last call of a newly redundant paradigm. TV is trusted by just 38% of viewers, compared with 77% who trust emails from friends. Read Don Tapscutt, who told you fifteen years ago at the same time as all those people - including me - started experimenting with how to make it so, that the world was irrevocably changing. You enjoy a platform that's not confined to a printed, out of date before it's proofed, ad rag. Your assertions and (witty, deeply acerbic) web logs reach, stimulate, annoy and amuse people you'll never meet (though as I said before, love to do this over a pint one day). Tens if not hundreds of millions of people now have a voice that can genuinely be heard. You too have been changed by the internet.

Enjoy your advertising. Enjoy the banners and viral films your world insisted on but which our new world thinks at best ephemerally amusing, at worst intrusive. Party hard while it lasts, because marketing changed while you were being funny. Enjoy the holiday weekend, perhaps upload something to Flickr.

The Ad Contrarian to Felix:

As usual, when confronted with a logical argument, a web maniac goes off into the stratosphere with every possible spurious irrelevancy.

I thought our conversation was about your assertion that the internet changed "everything, utterly." I understand why you would want to change the subject rather than defend such a preposterous position, but at least pretend to stay on subject.

Your argument is not an argument—it is merely another grab bag of unsubstantiated assertions, just like your first comment. There is only one fact in your comment: TV is trusted by 38% of viewers. What you neglect to say, however, is that the LEAST trusted of all major media is your precious internet.

I'm afraid your latest comment is quite typical of a new class of people who . . ."fly gliders, ride horses, have friends all over the world, throw parties, eat at nice restaurants, drive sports cars" and have no fucking idea how real people in the real world have to wash floors, change diapers, struggle to make payments on their refrigerators and don't spend all day having fucking conversations about fucking brands with their fucking "followers" on fucking Twitter.

And one more thing. I may have a float in the pomposity parade but, dude, you're the grand marshall.

Felix to The Ad Contrarian:

Very funny, I laughed out loud.

I grew up with my share of challenges, and my first job was as a washer-upper, but I've clearly matured into a passionate, pompous man—I should be in advertising. Oh, that's your gig, remember?

The internet isn't a single medium, like TV, it's a venue. 60% of people trust online peer recommendation—but unlike Oprah's book reviews this is actually peer to peer. That's the change. TV offers no peer communication, unless you'd like to cite Big Brother or Jerry Springer.

You and I may be gaudy cheerleaders in the grand pomposity parade (nice pompoms brother), but we're just at different ends of a spectrum that's both necessary and interesting. I happen to think one-way shouting is old, tired and in need of merciful release, and you may think the internet and its attendant democratisation of thought is just so much white noise (like, probably, this little debate), but there's no escaping the fact that it even changed you.

The existence of the net means that valid or invalid opinions can be aired and repeated, no matter if they come from a disenfranchised untouchable or a total ignoramus or a prince or an advertising guru. It means people can find common ground with others in a way never before possible. It means that no longer is that common ground office politics or the television soap or political propaganda everyone saw last night—it means the common ground is whatever anyone wants it to be. Opinion can be aired and can mobilise itself on a vast scale, evolving the views of hundreds of millions. TV only did that in 1963 or 1969 (and, to be fair, when Neighbours went global). You talk scathingly of my lack of appreciation for the man on the Clapham omnibus. To go back to the very beginning, bollocks man.

The internet is truly democratic in its reach; the UK has even recently asserted bandwidth for all as a right. This kind of universal access to global conversation is as revolutionary as universal suffrage, for the same reasons: it gives everyone a voice. Television, on the other hand, gives everyone entertainment. My esteemed sparring partner, the two are not equivalent, there is no competition between the two. One is new, one is old. If you had to get rid of one, even you know you'd choose to consign television to history.

The Ad Contrarian to Felix:
Somehow you have turned this conversation into a debate over TV versus the internet. I am not an apologist for TV. I've made no

claims for TV. You're arguing with yourself.

I don't give a shit about TV. I am just interested in facts.

When you claim that the internet has changed "everything, utterly" you have a responsibility to your readers (and to yourself) to be clear about how this is so. Just re-hashing assertions is the argument of a 10-year-old.

Here's the deal, Felix.

You seem like a nice, intelligent fellow whose brain has been addled by paying far too much attention to trendy nonsense.

You need to reconcile all the bullshit you read on line with the facts on the ground.

I want you to spend one hour in front of your local supermarket today and ask shoppers the following question:

"Before you came here today, did you consult the internet or have an online conversation with a friend about any of the brands you bought?"

Then maybe you can get your head out of your ass and see how the real world works.

Felix to The Ad Contrarian:

Yes dear. If you ask them while standing outside Tesco, they'll say no. But a million of them in the UK will be buying the stuff Tesco offered them as a special via email the day before, based on what their Clubcard recorded in their basket the previous week.

If you stand outside Boots they'll also say no, but they'll nonetheless have some Dove products in their basket because listening to the net built that brand.

You're being disingenuous, Bob. We're talking about marketing. The net changed marketing, because it's now about listening not asking, serving not telling.

And if you stand outside Amazon, or Dell, you'll fall off.

The Ad Contrarian to Felix:

So now spam email is your glorious "revolutionary global conversation." It's just fucking electronic coupons.

You gotta be fucking kidding.

Anyway, I'm tired of this so I'm going to give you the last word, go ahead . . .

Felix to The Ad Contrarian:

Yep, sorry mate, world changed while you were in broadcast mode.

Seriously and now that's all over, you might like 'Groundswell', pretty robust thinking from Forrester Research, though you might take issue with some of their rather unrefined segmentation.

THE FACEBOOK ENIGMA

An online article from *The Wall Street Journal* yesterday called "Valuing Facebook's Ads" reinforces the nagging doubts I have about the value of advertising on Facebook.

Amazingly, Facebook has a 24 share of all display advertising on the web. This is more than twice the share of its next rival.

The problem, though, is that it only has a 9.5 share of display advertising dollars.

In other words, advertisers want to be on Facebook, but they don't want to pay much for it. In fact, they are only willing to pay less than half of what they pay for an "average" display ad.

". . . Several agencies put the average price of an ad on Facebook in the U.S. in the $2 to $8 range for a thousand views . . The price is lower than the average $15 that other premium media sites can charge."

One thing we know for sure is that Facebook is enormously popular. What we don't know, however, is its value as an advertising medium.

". . . some marketers continue to question whether consumers pay attention to ads on social-networking sites, and wonder how effective they are in getting people to, say, buy cars."

The idiot wing of the ad business just naturally assumes that because Facebook has 50 zillion members it must be a good advertising medium. People with brains say, it's nice that you have all these members, but is it any good for advertising?

If, like me, you have serious doubts about Facebook as an ad medium, the numbers from the *Wall Street Journal* article only deepen your skepticism.

HOW SOCIAL MEDIA CONTROLS EVERYTHING

A reader has written to me and said,

Dear Ad Contrarian,

I go to marketing meetings every day. Often there are very bewildering Powerpoint slides presented. Just between you and me, I have no idea what these slides mean. But all my bosses keep nodding their heads and saying, "Hmm, that's interesting."

I am afraid that if I don't have pretty slides to present soon, I'm going to be thrown out of the marketing department and sent to a department where people have to work.

Can you help me?

Misty in Sunnyvale

Yes, Misty, I think I can help

In the world of marketing, the super-best subject to have complicated slides about is social media. If you have perplexing slides about social media, not only will you be admired and respected by friends and colleagues, you will also be considered an expert. Then, anytime someone has a question about social media, you can just make something up. It's the law!

I have created a nice slide about social media for you. I have used pictures and boxes and arrows and dotted lines and colors and even more arrows. Not only will this impress your bosses, it will also prepare you for a lifetime of brain-damaging Powerpoint presentations. You can find it on the next page.

Oh, and if anyone questions the validity of anything on this slide all you need to do is adopt your best condescending voice and say, "You just don't get it, do you."

How Social Media Controls Everything

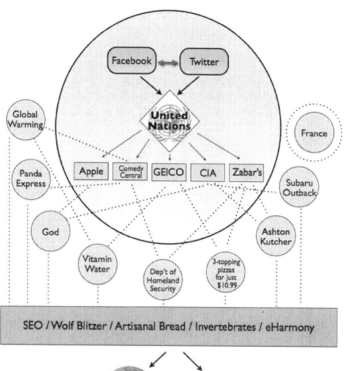

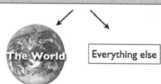

THE TRUE COST OF SOCIAL MEDIA

The great thing about social media is that it is a way for nimble brands to do significant, effective marketing without spending tons of money. Right?

Please, don't make me laugh.

Just for the heck of it, let's take a look at the 28 most popular brands on Facebook and see what they have in common.

1. Starbucks	15. Nutella
2. Coca Cola	16. Dr. Pepper
3. Oreo	17. Monster Energy
4. Skittles	18. Adidas
5. Red Bull	19. H&M
6. Victoria's Secret	20. Ferraro Rocher
7. Disney	21. McDonald's
8. Converse	22. Playstation
9. iTunes	23. XBox
10. MTV	24. Taco Bell
11. Zara	25. Puma
12. Pringles	26. BMW
13. NBA	27. Blackberry
14. Starburst	28. Nike

Notice anything?

A couple are cult brands. But in the overwhelming majority of cases, they are brands with enormous traditional marketing budgets.

This doesn't just apply to Facebook.

As *Forbes.com* reported, Anita Alberse, who teaches at Harvard Business School, found . . .

"*. . . The new world of social media may be a lot like the old world, if not more so . . .*

. . . videos that got watched the most on the Internet are those that bought their popularity through traditional offline advertising, especially on TV."

One of the dangerous things about social media is that it gives a certain type of incompetent marketing person unprecedented opportunities to pretend they're doing marketing when they're actually doing little of value. Here at *Ad Contrarian* World Headquarters, we call this "alibi advertising."

They can create spreadsheets that show 52 weeks of social media and convince the gullible and the foolish that something wonderful is going on.

People who believe that social media is a low-cost highway to marketing success are living in a digital dream world. They are either too naive to know, or too deceitful to tell their bosses, that with few exceptions there is a high cost to social media success.

It's called traditional advertising.

VALUE OF A FACEBOOK FAN

This weekend I had the misfortune of reading a mind-numbing piece of work called "The Value Of A Facebook Plan: An Empirical Review" by a company called Syncapse.

I knew this report would be a lot of bluff and bananas when I saw the word "empirical" in the title.

Syncapse modestly describes itself as "a global leader in the areas of community building, technology solutions, and digital measurement." Is that all? Not world peace or quantum thermodynamics?

The study purports to calculate the value of a Facebook fan. But it's riddled with problems. One of which is the problem of correlation versus causality.

People not trained in research or logic often have trouble understanding the difference between correlation and causality.

Here's a quick explanation.

If you were to study people who are hard-of-hearing you would probably find that they also have a much higher incidence of baldness. Does this mean that bad hearing causes baldness? Of course not. It occurs because old age causes both hearing and hair loss. So there is a correlation between deafness and baldness, but there is no causality. One does not cause the other.

Syncapse clearly shows that there is a connection between Facebook fanhood and certain financial and marketing benefits to a brand. But to demonstrate that Facebook fanhood has value, they need to show that the connection is causal, not just a correlation.

In other words, it is clear that to a particular brand a user who is a Facebook fan is worth more than an average user. But it is not clear that this has anything to do with being a Facebook fan. It may just be that Facebook fans are typical brand heavy users and that all heavy users are more valuable, whether they are Facebook fans or not.

In order to show that Facebook fanhood has value, Syncapse needs to demonstrate that "fanning" on Facebook actually causes higher value and doesn't just correlate with it. Which they have not done.

You might expect ignorant knuckleheads like you and me to confuse correlation with causality. But a "global leader in . . . digital measurement?" I'm shocked!

After 18 pages of charts and graphs and marketing babble that occasionally resembles English, Syncapse concludes that the average value of a Facebook fan is $136.38.

Not $137.12 or $135.29, but $136.38.

They do this through a series of calculations. As they say . . .

"Understanding long-term Facebook fan value is a complex undertaking with advanced calculations required across multiple variables."

But before doing advanced calculations across multiple variables, you first need a clue about what you're calculating.

The problem with the quantitative part of their study is that the underlying assumption they are using is wrong. It is based on . . .

". . . the measureable (sic) differences between (Facebook) users who have "fanned" a brand and those who have not."

Here's what's wrong with this assumption. If people who wear Red Sox caps spend $250 a year more with the Red Sox than people who don't, does that mean the value of a Red Sox cap is $250? Of course not. You are taking the value of the customer and attributing it to his hat. But that's essentially the logic of the Syncapse study.

They are taking the added value they've calculated for a Facebook fan and attributing it to Facebook at the expense of all other possible explanations.

Let's start at the beginning and pretend for a moment that, unlike Syncapse, we are not "global leaders in . . . digital measurement," we're just a bunch of bozos trying to figure out what a Facebook fan is worth.

We'll start with another example. After doing some calculations, Taco Bell finds that people who have Taco Bell bumper stickers are worth $100 a year more to them than people who don't have bumper stickers. The bumper sticker people buy more stuff at Taco Bell and they recommend it to their friends, etc.

Someone not very good at math or logic might conclude that this proves that a Taco Bell bumper sticker has a value to Taco Bell of $100.

Someone with a little more gray matter, might think differently. She might do another calculation and find that *all* Taco Bell customers (whether they have bumper stickers or not) are worth $95 a year more than people without Taco Bell bumper stickers. She might conclude that $95 of the $100 attributed to the bumper sticker actually comes from the fact that the person is a Taco Bell customer. She might conclude that the value of the bumper sticker is actually $5 a year.

So the key question for Syncapse is, how much of their imputed value can we attribute to "Facebook fan-ing" and how much to something else—like the fact that fans are more likely to be customers?

The answer is, I don't know and neither does Syncapse. And until they know, it is impossible for them to calculate a reliable value for a fan, no matter how many charts and graphs they produce.

It is my contention that a substantial part of the value imputed to being a Facebook fan has nothing to do with Facebook, and may be related to being either a customer or an active category participant or something else.

If I am right, Facebook fanhood has a far smaller value than the one they have calculated. This, of course, is not good for companies like Syncapse who have a vested interest in pumping up social media.

Apparently, when it came time to publish this study, someone at Syncapse with functioning synapses (sorry) must have read the thing and realized the fallacy of the logic. Buried on page 15 is the following disclaimer . . .

"It is important to note that this audience would still have value without Facebook . . ."

In other words, what they probably have been measuring is the value of the customer, not the value of his baseball cap.

ZEALOTS, MANIACS, AND HUSTLERS

Here at *The Ad Contrarian* Global Headquarters, we've developed a reputation for being anti-digital media and pro-traditional media. We are neither.

We have no personal interest in, or allegiance to, any medium.

Our only purpose is to fight bullshit, hyperbole and words without meaning. We are against zealots, maniacs and hustlers of any stripe.

Yes, we are vociferous in denouncing people who tell us that . . .

- traditional advertising is dead
- television is dead
- there is a new species of consumer that no longer needs to be persuaded
- the web has "changed everything"

Our aversion to this stuff is not based on ideology, it is based on data. There is no evidence at all that any of this is true, and there is plenty of evidence to the contrary.

We would be equally vociferous in our denunciations if traditional media hustlers were saying that . . .

- digital marketing is dead
- the web is dead
- there is a new species of consumer that no longer shares information about products
- TV has "changed everything"

As a matter of fact, you will find that we have been just as voluble in our disdain for the "brand babbler" wing of traditional advertising as we are for cult members of *The Divine Church of The Internet.*

There are many smart, reasonable people working in digital media who do not make preposterous assertions; who do not think that social media is the answer to every question; who do not speak in dreadful, impenetrable jargon.

We respect and appreciate these people.

All we want to do is get our readers to understand:

- the risks and rewards of all media investments
- the difference between facts and "buzz"
- that success stories (both digital and traditional) tend to find their way into print but failures get buried
- that the "narrative" that has arisen about social media marketing is largely anecdotal and substantially fact-free.

We try not to be advocates of anything other than common sense. We try not to be enemies of anything other than bullshit.

Chapter 5

Brand Babble and Marketing Madness

YOU'VE GOT A BRAND PROBLEM

There was a time in America when every problem was a "communications" problem.

If you couldn't get along with your husband, you weren't communicating. If your kid was incorrigible, you probably couldn't "get through" to him. If your boss didn't like you, you weren't "on the same wavelength." There seemed to be no problems of substance, just problems of communication.

Well, the truth is, sometimes your husband is just a pain in the ass, and your kid is a nasty little brat, and your boss thinks you're a worthless shit. And all the communication in the world won't help. In fact, it will usually hurt.

Today we have the business version of this. Instead of communication, the catch-all problem in marketing is "the brand." So if your products are crappy, or your stores are dirty, or your service is lousy, or your business strategy is stupid, you, my friend, have a "brand" problem! Call in the branding consultants. Pay them a few hundred thou and let them study your brand for a few months.

You see, solving real problems requires unpleasantness. Systems have to be changed. Products have to be redesigned. People have to be fired. Floors have to be swept and walls have to be painted.

Brand tinkering, on the other hand, is generally quite agreeable. All it requires is money and a bunch of congenial meetings. Hire some branding consultants. Appoint a task force. Interview "stakeholders". Conduct focus groups. Have an off-site or two at a nice hotel.

Then start reporting the "learnings." Fire up the Powerpoint projector. Share the results. But remember, everyone's point of view is valid!

Best of all, if there's any real work to be done, it will be done by the consultants who'll give you a nice fat report filled with charts and graphs and the latest up-to-the-minute buzzwords and cliches to quibble over for months. And if anyone asks what you're doing about the problems you can make a lovely little presentation.

Tinkering with "the brand" is so much more pleasant than fixing the problems. But, unfortunately, after the money is spent and the naval-gazing brand babblers have gone home, someone still has to sweep the floor and paint the walls.

WHY CAN'T MARKETERS TALK STRAIGHT?

I sometimes play a game. As I'm walking down a street, I look at how people are dressed and divide them into two categories: those who are trying to stand out, and those who are trying to fit in.

I do a similar thing when I interview people. I listen to their language and analyze whether they are trying to cloud or clarify.

One way we can tell that the marketing and advertising industries are in dire straits is by listening to the language.

From the HP website:

". . . (HP's) collaborative approach is tailored to a customer's ecosystem to create adaptive infrastructures that use leading software products and architectures and leverage HP's own expertise in the creation of adaptive infrastructures."

Oh.

Spend time at a conference, read a trade publication, listen to a presentation and it soon becomes obvious that speaking plainly and clearly has become anathema to most marketing practitioners.

Instead, we have developed an appalling lexicon of contrived phrases and dreadful gibberish meant to confuse rather than elucidate.

Our most popular words have vague meanings and fuzzy definitions—branding, engagement, conversation . . .

It's my belief that a sure sign of a deteriorating discipline is that the participants have agreed on a system of imprecise discourse to replace clear thoughts and exact meanings.

On the value of speaking plainly, Einstein once said, "It should be possible to describe the laws of physics to a barmaid."

One of my heroes is Richard Feynman. Feynman was a genius. He was a Nobel prize winning physicist, he translated Mayan hieroglyphics, he uncovered the cause of the Challenger disaster, was a best-selling author, a bongo player, and an all-around nut. As brilliant as he was, he hated complicated, imprecise language. He once defined "hypothesis" as "a fancy word for a guess."

By the way, Feynman went to Far Rockaway High School, where so many of America's great thinkers were educated.

THE MOST POWERFUL FORCE IN MARKETING

Think of all the amazing new products that have been introduced in the past few years.

In the digital realm alone, there have been thousands of them. Every day I stumble on new offerings on the web that I had no idea existed that amaze me with their utility and creativity.

The startling fact, however, is how few of them become successful businesses.

The reason so many new products and new ideas do not succeed is a function of human psychology—the reluctance of people to do something new and different. Most companies either don't understand this or choose to ignore it.

Marketers always overestimate the attractiveness of new things and always underestimate the power of traditional consumer behavior.

I have been involved in the development of many new products and a lot of advertising campaigns for new products. Almost every new product I've been associated with has been either a reasonably good idea or an improvement on what went before. But most weren't compelling enough to overcome consumer attachment to doing what they usually do.

One of the biggest mistakes a marketer can make is taking too seriously what consumers say about a product in the development stage. When consumers are exposed to it, they will tell you it's a good idea. But what they can never tell you is whether it's a good enough idea to eclipse the inertia of their habits.

The most powerful force in marketing is not price, quality, distribution, advertising, or branding—it's the resistance to change.

THE AGE OF THE COMPLICATOR

"There are a lot of great technicians in advertising. And unfortunately they talk the best game. They know all the rules . . . They can give you fact after fact after fact. They are the scientists of advertising. But there's one little rub. Advertising is fundamentally persuasion and persuasion happens to be not a science, but an art." Bill Bernbach, 1947

As advertising and marketing have become more sophisticated, more technologically advanced, and more populated with well-trained specialists, we are constantly reminded by clients that it has also become less effective.

We blame the problem on environmental issues—clutter, disengaged consumers, proliferation of media. Anything but us.

But the problem is systemic. We've lost our way. We are no longer clear on the purpose of advertising. We have invented a whole culture of obfuscation and a catalog of false goals.

We want to engage consumers. We want to have conversations with consumers. We want to have relationships with consumers. And in the process, we have forgotten the essential purpose of advertising—to persuade consumers.

So how do we bring advertising back down to Earth?

First, we have to remove the word "branding" from our vocabulary. It has lost its meaning and has become a catch-all cliche to justify pretty much anything we can convince a client to spend money on. Someone please tell me one thing you can't put a client's logo on and call it "branding."

Next we have to realize that successful brands are by-products. They don't come about by "branding." They come about by doing lots of other things well. Like making great products; satisfying our customers; differentiating our products in advertising.

Then we have to understand that the most efficient, most effective, most durable way to build a brand is to *sell someone something*. Experiencing a product is a thousand times more powerful than experiencing an ad. Getting someone to try your product is far and away the best way to build your brand.

It is also the most efficient way to engage consumers, have conversations with them, and build a relationship with them. The engagement/conversation/relationship crowd are confused about cause and effect. You don't sell someone something by engagement, conversation and relationship. You create engagement, conversation and relationships by selling them something.

Which leads us back to the simple art of advertising. We are not anthropologists, sociologists or psychologists. We are creative people. We have to get all the sidewalk psychologists, all the jargon-babbling planners, all the anthropologists-without-shovels out of the way.

We have to clear out all the human speed-bumps and detour signs. We don't need more strategists. We need better creative people.

We have to identify and hire a new generation of creative people and let them do what they do best—charm and persuade.

We are salesmen. Get used to it.

BUMMER FOR MARKETERS: WE GOTTA DO SOMETHING

Stop the presses!

According to an article in Ad Age last week called *Why Measurement Alone Will Not Lead To Better Marketing,* things don't automatically get better because we measure them. Apparently, to make things better, we have to do something.

What a bummer.

I guess this means that taking your temperature doesn't make your flu go away. And a longer tape measure will not make you taller.

Damn, nothing's easy anymore.

I can't believe these guys expect us to do something? We can't just drool all over the metrics? We can't just collect data and make spread sheets and print up reports?

We have to think? And have ideas? And do things?

In order to reach their brilliant conclusion, the authors interviewed 400 CEOs, CFOs and CMOs. I swear, this is not a joke.

I think many of us could have figured this out after interviewing four puppy dogs and a cheese grater.

Frankly, I don't think this study will sit well at all with marketers. If there's one thing we marketers hate to do, it's something.

BRANDING'S FINAL ABSURDITY

There's very little fun left in the ad business, but one of the big chuckles we still get (secretly) is watching our clients go through idiotic "branding" exercises.

These con games last for months, cost hundreds of thousands of dollars, and generally have less impact on business than cleaning the drapes.

Nonetheless, there are very clever companies out there making zillions of dollars convincing businesses that all they need to do is "fix their brand" and all will be well.

I can only compare the pain of participating in one of these exercises to putting on ski boots and watching *Cats*.

Now branding has reached the height of absurdity. The U.K. has embarked on a re-branding program. This is not a joke.

Part of the process, introduced by Prime Minister Gordon Brown's government, is to find out "what does it mean to be British?" Well, Gordo, it used to mean you had an empire to run. Now it apparently means you have nothing better to do than sit on your fat ass and engage in the same type of moronic navel-gazing usually reserved for overfed CMO's.

To poke fun at this idea, the cynics at *The Times* of London sponsored a slogan-writing contest for their readers for a new British "brand." My favorite entry: "At Least We're Not French."

A representative of the British government said that after writing a "statement of values", the government would . . . hold "an extensive and intensive" period of consultation with regular citizens on what being British means to them. Then it will convene a "citizens' summit" of 500 to 1,000 people who will "deliberate on the matter."

Get out the ski boots.

SCIENTISTS DISCOVER THE BRAND GENE

"Brand affinity is clearly hard wired. It is . . . fundamental to human existence. It must have a genetic component." Google CEO, Eric Schmidt

NEW YORK - In a paper published today, researchers from the University of Search Engine Optimization claim to have discovered the brand gene.

For years geneticists have speculated that humans must have a "brand gene." How else, they say, can you explain the success of Meineke Mufflers and Pillsbury Toaster Strudel?

The article claims that the brand gene first appeared about 200,000 years ago in sub-Saharan Africa and helped our species develop language, social skills, and really cool sunglasses.

Anthropologists speculate that previously there was another species of human-like primates that did not have the brand gene. These proto-humans walked upright and developed primitive tools, but couldn't tell Jif from Skippy, and believed Evian and Crystal Geyser were pretty much the same stuff. Scientists marvel at their survival.

Geneticists say that through a chance mutation, one individual was born with the brand gene.

This individual had a huge advantage over others of his species. While others walked around cluelessly in Gap apparel, he felt an affinity for Abercrombie and Fitch. He drove a wicked cool Pontiac Vibe instead of his father's Honda Civic.

They speculate that in short order members of this new species had swooshes on their hunting clubs and little alligator logos on their animal skins. This attracted others of their group and led to lots of super-hot cave sex and a thriving new species.

Scientists have named this newly discovered species "Nebranderthal Man" *(Homo nebranderthalensis.)*

It wasn't long before Nebranderthal Man made it out of Africa, to Tribeca and Santa Monica where brands of greater and greater complexity were developed.

Today, scientists are devising tests to help those born with defective brand genes. These people can often be seen wearing a Hard Rock Cafe t-shirt or driving a Mitsubishi Galant. To help these people, activists are calling for universal brand gene screening.

Scientists claim that because we now know the genetic basis for brand affinity, they are beginning to understand previously unexplained phenomena, like the existence of Panda Express and Cool Ranch Doritos.

Today's report adds fuel to the ongoing disagreement between those who believe branding is a fundamental component of human existence—like eating, breathing, sex and shoplifting—and those who believe it's just a load of marketing bullshit.

SCOTS ON THE ROCKS

Not long ago, when you arrived at an airport in Scotland, you were greeted by signs and posters announcing that you were visiting *"The Best Small Country In The World."*

According to *The Times* of London *". . . this was the slogan of Jack McConnell, the previous First Minister, and it was derided by Alex Salmond when he was elected First Minister in May. In the new era of nationalism, the time seemed ripe for inspiring words that might evoke romance and expectation as much as they promised modernity and brisk efficiency."*

So, after spending $250,000 and six months, the new administration recently rolled out its inspiring, romantic new slogan at Scotland's airports:

"Welcome to Scotland"

DEATH BY BRANDING

Southwest Airlines better be careful. They have been a great example of how the best way to build a brand is with *product* advertising. They are now on the road to proving how the best way to kill a brand is with branding.

Here we have an airline that offers about the worst flying experience in the nation. But they haven't wasted their money trying to make us love them. Instead, they have wisely spent their money getting us to *fly* them.

They have given us specific, concrete reasons to fly with them: lower fares, more flights, more convenient destinations. As a result, they have actually built a meaningful brand—a brand that stands for something concrete and discernible—while United and American, et al, with all their "brand" advertising, stand for nothing.

But lately Southwest's advertising has the smell of "branding" all over it. They are trying to change our attitudes about them. Good luck.

What makes their new campaign so awful is that they're trying to convince business travelers that flying Southwest will make us more "productive." Right. That's the big airline issue for me. Not price. Not schedule. Not comfort. Not reliability.

"Bob, what airline you wanna take?"

"I don't know. Which one makes me more productive?"

It's such a moronic strategy, it can only have come from a trained marketing professional.

As a service to the marketing department at Southwest, I thought I'd give them one traveler's list of the top 10 things he considers when choosing an airline:

1. Hope I don't die.
2. Hope I get an upgrade.
3. Hope the toilet ain't too stinky.
4. Hope I don't sit next to a talker.
5. Hope it leaves on time.

6. Hope I don't sit next to a laptop maniac.
7. Hope I don't sit next to a smelly fatty.
8. Hope I don't sit next to a smelly fatty laptop maniac talker.
9. Hope I don't die.
10. Hope I don't die.

ACCOUNT PLANNERS GONE WILD

Recently, an article appeared in *Ad Age* about a new Volvo ad campaign. The article described how Volvo's ad agency developed the idea for its new campaign.

Apparently, the agency interviewed valet car parkers to find out what Volvo drivers are like. I swear this is not a joke. Valet car parkers.

I wonder what planning genius came up with this idea.

Volvo enjoyed many deep insights about their owners from this exercise.

"They are users not havers; they use what they have," says the agency's account director.

Apparently the rest of us don't use what we have. I know I haven't been using what I have lately.

Volvo's Director of Global Advertising added,

"Safety is about enhancing the quality of life for people inside and outside the car."

Uh . . . excuse me, moron. Safety is about saving your kids' lives, okay?

According to the article,

'The results were enough to build a campaign showing Volvo drivers as "we" people as opposed to "me" people.'

To this I would just like to add, Give Me A Fucking Break!

I know agencies are brilliant at coming up with this bullshit, but what kind of nitwit client actually believes it?

This account planning thing has gotten way out of control. We've got to kill them all and start over.

BRAND BABBLE MEETS DIGI-DRIVEL

A few weeks ago I wrote, "we have to remove the word branding from our vocabulary. It has lost its meaning . . ."

If you need further evidence, I urge you to read *Time To Rewrite The Brand Playbook For Digital* in *Ad Age* this week.

It's been a long time since I've enjoyed a piece of highfalutin' baloney as much as I enjoyed this thing.

The author, of course a "digital strategist," managed to use the word "brand" or some derivative of it 54 times in a 58-sentence article. That's a brand babble quotient of .93 which is a new world's indoor record. Kudos all around!

She has also been able to do a lovely job of integrating brand babble with digital gibberish to come up with a true tour de force of contemporary marketing double talk. A few excerpts . . .

"Instead of simply wondering whether we should spend more time and effort on developing strategy or focusing on implementation, our challenge is to address branding online simultaneously as behavior and technology."

Note to self: Darn it, stop wasting all that time wondering whether we should spend more time and effort on developing strategy or focusing on implementation.

"There's always an opportunity to choose anew how a brand is going to behave online."

And if it doesn't behave online, no dessert. I mean it!

"The branding industry of the past worked by coming up with an idea that they handed off. In the branding industry of the present, it is not easy to hand things off."

And in the branding industry of the future, there will be no hand-offs. It will be all passing. Everyone go long.

". . . people's behavior in digital is shaped by a simple trade-off between expected gains and expected costs of interacting with a brand."

Really? I thought people's behavior in digital was shaped by watching too many naughty videos.

"*Traditional branding deals with extending the brand promise to the digital space and integrating go-to-market tactics with digital tactics to support the brand promise.*"

How many times have we all said that!

"*Of course, brands realized that they needed to appropriate their message to the new media, according to McLuhan's "medium is the message" idea, and now everyone is talking about brand experiences online.*"

Poor Marshall. He takes the rap for so many knuckleheads

SEA KITTEN STATE PARK

PETA (People for the Ethical Treatment of Animals) thinks we are too cruel to fish. They think we would treat fish more kindly if instead of calling them "fish" we started calling them "sea kittens."

This is not a joke.

Because of the budget deficit in California, the state is planning to close a bunch of state parks including one called Pescadero State Beach. Pescadero means "place to go fishing."

PETA have offered to pay to keep the beach open if the state will agree to change the name from "Pescadero State Beach" to "Sea Kitten State Park."

You simply cannot make this shit up.

I'M TIRED OF STRATEGISTS

I'm sick and tired of strategists.

Can you please send me some people who can do things, not talk about them.

Da Vinci didn't need a strategist. Neither did Newton. Or Einstein. Or Gershwin. Or Hitchcock. Or Riney, for that matter.

They just did brilliant things. They didn't need people chattering at them about what they should do or how they should do it. They just did it.

I'm tired of business strategists.

And marketing strategists.

And advertising strategists.

And media strategists

And web strategists.

And social media strategists.

And editorial strategists.

And content strategists.

I'm tired of people who know how to do everyone's job but their own, and ad agencies who know how to run everyone's business but their own.

This industry needs more doers. We have more than enough chatterers.

NONSENSE NEVER SLEEPS

When will these morons ever learn?

I read a post on a website called Business Insider recently entitled *The Brick-And-Mortar Retail Store Is Headed For Extinction.* I thought I was in some kind of stupidity time warp.

This is the same nonsense I was reading 15 years ago. It was bullshit then, and it's even stinkier bullshit now.

The article was written by some guy who claims to be "Managing Director at a $2 billion venture capital firm based in NYC." Remind me not to venture any capital with this guy.

Here's a sample of his logic:

". . . My partner Larry told me about one innovative retailer that uses their physical store to crowd source and showcase new products only—as soon as something sells in meaningful volume . . . it is moved to the online store and that shelf space is freed for a new product to experience."

Now there, my friend, is some brilliant marketing! Take all the good-selling stuff *out* of the store and only leave the crap that no one wants.

Hey, Steve, wake up! Take all those iPhones and iPads and iPods out of your stores and make people go online to buy them, you idiot. That way you won't have all that annoying store traffic. Instead, you could be putting in some crap that nobody wants. Maybe Gates has some old Zunes laying around.

Or even better, you can get some slow selling crowdsourced stuff—ohmygod, double wicked cool—crowdsourced!

Then there's this statement..

"Over time, I see stores being "owned" by marketing and viewed it as a brand expense instead of the independent full P&L today."

Apparently there is a language in which that sentence makes sense. But I'm afraid you need two billion dollars to understand it.

SOMEBODY PLEASE EXPLAIN

I rarely criticize other agency's work. It's too easy to be a creative genius/cheap shot artist when you don't have to deal with the problems or the clients.

But I have to say, Wendy's recent campaign has me completely baffled. The campaign theme is this:

"It's waaaay better than fast food. It's Wendy's."

Here's why I'm confused:

Everyone in the world, except apparently Wendy's, knows that it *is* fast food.

The 30% of the population who eat almost all the fast food, really *like* fast food.

So the question is:

Why would you say it's not fast food when everyone knows it is?

And why would you insult your customer base by denigrating something they like?

They can't possibly believe they can build their business by targeting non-fast food users, can they? No one's that stupid. So what's going on?

It seems to me there's only one explanation for a strategy this cockeyed—the tortured logic of account planning.

I can just hear the presentation.

"We spent 3 months living with Wendy's customers, bathing with them, and helping them spank their children. Our unique insight is that even though they visit fast food restaurants twelve times a day, their body language tells us they have tremendous feelings of guilt and self-hatred . . . they want the reality of fast food, but not the idea of fast food . . . we can differentiate the Wendy's brand by disassociating Wendy's from fast food . . ."

Of course, I'm just making this up. But I wonder how far off it is?

MORONS AND THEIR MONEY

Stop the presses! Here's some huge news. Consumers favor brands that offer them good quality at a low price! Oh my god!

"The 26,000 men and women polled . . . showed a strong inclination to brands that either saved them money or were perceived as having good value" is how Brandweek reported it.

A company called Brand Keys did the survey. Apparently, they had to poll 26,000 people to figure this out. You think we could have saved them some money?

But wait. There's more. Just the name of the survey tells you it was done by nitwits: The *"2007 Brand Keys Customer Loyalty Engagement Leaders List"* is what it's called.

Congratulations to Brand Keys on squeezing every horrible cliche and buzzword in the marketing lexicon into one survey title. A masterful achievement.

Oh, and one more thing—a warning to anyone who uses the word "engagement." I'm going to come after you. I mean it.

BRAND BABBLE BATTLES BACK

So far, 2011 has been a very good year for web-monkey *jargonistas*. But we've been uncharacteristically short on brand babble.

As a matter of fact, I was starting to think that under the relentless pressure of social media claptrap, the whole art of brand babble was losing steam.

I am happy to report, however, that a treasure trove of recent brand babble has been unearthed. It's an article called *10 Ways Your Brand Can Be Meaningful*. Everything about it is delicious.

First of all, it's found at the perfect spot—a website called *CMO. com*. You couldn't ask for better provenance than that.

Second, it's written by someone who's a partner in *Emotive Brand*. Now, to be honest here, I have no idea who or what *Emotive Brand* is. For all I know, they're a fine group of wonderful people. But if the name doesn't make you cringe, you've been in marketing way too long.

And third, it provides us with an excellent vision of the future of marketing jargon. It manages to create a lovely amalgam of classical brand babble, sociological double-talk, and new age digi-drivel.

The article is deeply concerned with the "meaning" of brands. In a true *tour de force,* using just two short pages, it manages to incorporate the word "meaning," or some derivative of it, 53 times.

Among its plenitude of platitudes, we are exhorted to . . .

"Take in more. Grow. Pursue new paths. Climb new mountains. Swim new seas. Cross new deserts. Plow new fields . . ."

Yup, I'll get right on that.

"It behooves your brand to move people to a new level of consciousness—about your brand, their own lives, and the connection between he two."

Really? Can't we just sell them stuff? Exactly what new level of consciousness has Mountain Dew taken us to? Or Miracle Whip? Or Flaming Hot Cheetos?

"The pursuit of meaning consolidates what's already there in the

abstract into something more tangible, more understood, more usable. With an agreed meaning, a brand starts to evolve into a meaningful brand."

Would someone please notify the tautology police.

"You are on the road to meaning. You roll down the windows and let fresh air replace the old, stagnant ways of the past. You put down the convertible top and see the big sky above. You step on the gas and feel how much easier it is now to move forward . . ."

. . . you put a loaded gun to your head and say, what in the world has this business come to?

MEET THE sChMO

There is a new variety of CMO I have encountered recently. Maybe you've met him.

- My title is CMO, but my job is advertising coordinator
- My primary responsibilities are to manage meetings and get approvals
- I always agree with the highest ranking person in the room
- My favorite topic is the great things we did at my last job
- The dumbest person in the world is the person who had my job before me
- The dumbest agency in the world is the agency she hired
- I am highly skilled at making pronouncements, but far less skilled at making decisions
- When I do make a decision, it rarely lasts more than 48 hours
- I am excellent at delegating responsibility. I am even better at delegating blame
- I manage the budget, but I don't control it
- I am an expert on using the latest marketing terminology
- I don't care if it's good, as long as it's "cutting edge"
- I am very well-groomed and very well-fed
- I will be here for 18 months
- I am a sChMO

THE ECO-MARKETING SCAM

Here at *Ad Contrarian* World Headquarters, we yield to no one in our appreciation of ducks and trees and bunnies.

However, we also harbor deep suspicions about people who make a public spectacle of their supposed dedication to environmental purity. As far as we're concerned, the philosophical underpinnings of a virtuous life can be summed up very briefly—do it and shut the fuck up.

Consequently, we are more than a little annoyed at the burgeoning movement toward environmental grandstanding by corporate America. We are happy that corporations are starting to feel responsible for the messes they create. But we are of the mind that cleaning-up after yourself is a fundamental responsibility that every 9-year old should learn. It's not a corporate extra credit project.

Of all the eco-bluster currently in vogue, the kind that really fries our eggs is the kind that hijacks the language of environmentalism, but has nothing at all to do with it.

Above you will see a little bit of cynical eco-babble we found in a hotel last week. You probably can't read the small print, but what it says is that by *not* using the double-headed shower apparatus they have installed we can "restore our world."

So here's what I want to know. If they're so concerned about restoring our world, why did they install these fucking wasteful, unnecessary shower heads to begin with?

Because they're phony, cynical bastards who are trying to have it both ways? I would never say such a thing, but a less magnanimous person might certainly draw that conclusion.

BOTTOM-UP BRANDING

If you need some motivation to stick a knife in your head, ask your average advertising whiz-kid about "brands."

He'll go on for weeks about brand integration and brand expectations and brand experiences and brand advocates and brand relevancy and brand messaging.

He knows everything there is to know about brand babble. And almost nothing about brand building.

Perhaps the most expensive and wasteful form of brand illiteracy is the "top-down" view of branding. This is typified by the style of advertising practiced by banks, life insurance companies, oil companies, investment houses and airlines who have no clue about differentiating themselves.

"Top-down" advertising is easy to identify. It usually has happy, generic people doing happy generic things while music plays and voices either sing or speak. There is little to nothing said about the specifics of what they do or make. It is full of promises and hopefulness. It tries to convince you that, heck, they're people, too, and you really ought to like them.

The "top-down" view is that if you just get the "branding" right everything else will fall into place. In most categories, this way of thinking results in a very costly public dialogue between an advertiser and himself.

Top-down branding works in a few categories—fashion, booze, cigarettes and some luxury goods. Account planners, marketing coordinators and others with limited vision think that because these are heavily advertised categories this is how advertising works in general.

In fact, about 95% of the stuff we buy is not fashion, booze, cigarettes or luxury goods. It's mayonnaise and toothbrushes and shower curtains and socks.

If you are not in the business of selling fashion, booze, cigarettes or luxury goods, you would be wise to forget about "brand" advertising and focus your ad dollars on differentiating your products.

The strongest brands are built "bottom-up"—by outstanding product advertising.

As we always say around *Ad Contrarian* headquarters, we don't get them to try our product by convincing them to love our brand. We get them to love our brand by convincing them to try our product.

Chapter 6

Myths and Magic

YOU AND ME AND MONKEYS THROWING DARTS

Here at *Ad Contrarian* World Headquarters, there are a few principles that guide us.

First, we never make predictions. The reason for this is that people who make predictions are almost always wrong. It's way more entertaining to make fun of other people's stupid predictions than to have them make fun of yours.

Another is that we never trust experts. Again, their pontifications almost always turn out wrong and there's nothing we like better than sticking it to them.

We try to base our opinions on facts rather than ideology. This is a point of view that is terribly out of fashion in contemporary marketing.

Just to clarify something here, there are certain types of experts we have vastly more confidence in than others. Physical scientists, while sometimes mistaken, have a system of checks and balances that self-corrects. They are constantly peer-testing each other's assertions, which in the fullness of time usually leads to the uncovering of fallacious ideas. Social scientists, on the other hand, are completely unreliable. They use the language and trappings of science, but their studies usually produce opinions, not facts.

Consequently, I believe experts in the physical sciences really are experts, while "experts" in the social sciences are frequently just people with credentials and noisy beliefs.

Of all the social sciences, economics is the one I have least confidence in. As George Bernard Shaw once famously said, "If all the economists were laid end to end, they'd never reach a conclusion." President Harry Truman, tired of hearing economists say, "On one hand . . . but on the other hand . . ." asked if anyone knew where he could find a one-handed economist.

Of the disciplines within economics, marketing is the one I have toiled in, am most familiar with and, sadly, have little confidence in.

While I believe that this field is laden with bozos and charlatans, the truth is I have no comprehensive scientific evidence to prove it. All I have are anecdotes. Anecdotes are fun, but unreliable.

This does not mean, however, that there isn't evidence in other disciplines that demonstrates the unreliability of many social science "experts."

Enter Philip Tetlock.

Tetlock is an author, professor of organizational behavior at the Haas Business School at the University of California-Berkeley, and the winner of lots of impressive awards.

According to CNN Tetlock is the world's foremost expert on experts. For over 25 years, he has been conducting an experiment to quantify the forecasting skill of political experts.

Tetlock has studied 300 academics, economists, policymakers and journalists and compared more than 82,000 of their forecasts to what actually happened in the real world. Here are his conclusions:

- "We found that our experts' predictions barely beat random guesses—the statistical equivalent of a dart-throwing chimp . . ."

- "Ironically, the more famous the expert, the less accurate his or her predictions tended to be."

- "(Experts) go wrong when they leap to judgment or are too slow to change their minds in the face of contrary evidence."

- "Partisans across the opinion spectrum are vulnerable to occasional bouts of ideologically induced insanity."

- "The most important factor was not how much education or experience the experts had but how they thought. You know the famous line that [philosopher] Isaiah Berlin borrowed from a Greek poet, "The fox knows many things, but the hedgehog knows one big thing"? The better forecasters were like Berlin's foxes: self-critical, eclectic thinkers who were willing to update their beliefs when faced with contrary evidence, were doubtful of grand schemes and were rather modest about their predictive ability. The less successful forecasters were like hedgehogs: They tended to have one big, beautiful idea that they loved to stretch, sometimes to the breaking point. They tended to be articulate and very persuasive as to why their idea explained everything. The media often love hedgehogs."

From a *New Yorker* article about Tetlock's book *Expert Political Judgment*:

- "When (experts are) wrong, they're rarely held accountable, and they rarely admit it, either. They insist that they were just off on timing, or blindsided by an improbable event, or almost right, or wrong for the right reasons."
- "The accuracy of an expert's predictions actually has an inverse relationship to his or her self-confidence, renown, and, beyond a certain point, depth of knowledge."
- "*Expert Political Judgment* is just one of more than a hundred studies that have pitted experts against statistical or actuarial formulas, and in almost all of those studies the people either do no better than the formulas or do worse."

Listening to Tetlock speak recently, I found one of his points particularly gratifying. He said that an algorithm that predicted no change did better than the experts in forecasting the future. This coincides nicely with a little aphorism that appears every day in the right column near the bottom of my blog, "Nobody ever got famous predicting that things would stay pretty much the same."

In advertising, we have always had a great many articulate, self-assured, and highly-esteemed people who pass themselves off as experts and futurists. As the art and technology of marketing have become more esoteric and arcane, and as data, metrics, and analytics have soared to the forefront of our attention, these people have achieved greater and greater status. Their pretensions are, once again, undercut by Tetlock.

"... *mathematics has a certain mystique. People get intimidated by it, and no one challenge(s) the models.*"

Most of our experts (and their acolytes) tend to be enthusiasts and ideologues. This makes them unreliable. Regardless of their credentials and their alarming self-regard, they are no better at forecasting trends or results than you or me or monkeys throwing darts.

Follow them at your peril.

IT'S A WONDERFUL WORLD

"Advertising is a failure. When you don't have that good relationship, then you have to advertise . . ." Jeff Jarvis

Did you know that Coca-Cola is failing? And Apple is failing and McDonald's is failing and Proctor and Gamble is failing?

You didn't know that? Where have you been?

It's obvious. They have to advertise. Advertising is what you have to do when you're failing.

This is because the internet has created a new species of human being. And these new human beings live in a wonderful world in which they have good relationships with all the companies that make the products they use.

The only time companies need to advertise to these people is when that relationship is broken and failing.

You see, these new humans don't buy things for practical reasons like, it works better, or it's cheaper, or it looks nicer. It's all about the relationship.

These new humans want a direct relationship with their peanut butter maker and their muffler manufacturer. They want a relationship with the company that makes their socks and their chairs. And their pickles, and their half-and-half, and their mayonnaise, and their cookies, and their tires, and their chewing gum, and their toothbrush, and their umbrella, and their dishwasher, and their napkins, and their toaster, and their gasoline, and their horseradish, and their dental floss, and their paper towels, and their golf balls, and their shoes, and their pillows, and their pencils, and their deodorant, and their books, and their nail clippers, and their furniture polish, and their frozen chicken strips, and their lamps, and their potting soil, and their bathing suits, and their glasses, and their clocks, and their fungicide, and their dishes, and their cat food, and their sun block, and their cookie dough, and their motor oil, and their light bulbs, and their burglar alarm, and their ironing board, and their fire insurance, and their coffee filters, and their pillow cases, and their allergy pills, and their mouthwash, and their vacuum cleaner bags, and their shower curtains . . .

So you needn't bother telling them that your product works better, or is cheaper, or looks nicer. That's just a sign of failure. It's just a sign that your relationship is failing.

These new humans live in a wonderful world. It's a world in which their minds are free to evaluate the relationships they have with all these companies. They don't have to worry about their jobs, or their children, or how they're going to pay the mortgage.

They don't need to wash their bath tubs, or have mammograms, or go to work, or apply for loans, or bail their kids out of juvenile hall, or fold the laundry, or take their parents to the doctor, or vacuum, or make dinner.

They have all the time in the world to develop direct relationships with companies. And then, when they're finished building these relationships, they go on line to social media sites and have conversations with and about these companies.

It's a wonderful world.

Someday I'd like to visit it

BRILLIANT AND DELUSIONAL

A very interesting ad guy named Tony Schwartz died this week. Tony was a strange and remarkable person.

Tony was responsible for the most famous political spot ever created, called the "Daisy Ad."

The spot was created for Lyndon Johnson during the presidential race of 1964. The spot was unquestionably one of the most brilliant —and slanderous—political ads ever run. And was hugely effective.

It implied that Barry Goldwater, Johnson's adversary, was dangerously irresponsible and was likely to trigger nuclear war. It was the granddaddy of all the awful, negative political advertising we are subject to today.

The thing that interests me most about Tony is something that interests me about a lot of artists—their blindness to the ramifications of their work. In Tony's words . . .

"For many years, it's been referred to as the beginning of negative commercials . . . There was nothing negative about it. Frankly, I think it was the most positive commercial ever made."

FIVE REASONS ACCOUNT PLANNING NEEDS TO DIE

As many regular readers of this blog know, I am a former science teacher turned copywriter, turned creative director, turned management bean counter.

Each of my incarnations has a little compartment in my brain. Consequently, I often look at ads like a science geek, or finances like a copywriter. It's very confusing, but it keeps me interested.

As a result of my background, I have a few prejudices. Before we rip into planning, let's get them out on the table:

I am highly skeptical of social sciences.

I am thoroughly tiresome on the question of what is a fact and what is an opinion-masquerading-as-a-fact.

I am a creative department chauvanist. I believe the creative department makes the advertising and everyone else makes the arrangements.

Now that you know my prejudices, let's get on with subject of today's rant.

I think it's time for account planning to crawl away and die. Here are five reasons why:

1. Strategy is too important to be left to the strategists. Advertising and brand strategy ought to be done by the smartest people at the agency. I don't care if their titles are art director, billing supervisor, or ceo. The most important thing an agency does is make ads—and the ads are usually worthless if the strategy isn't right. In my experience, the ability to synthesize an imaginative strategy is unrelated to job title. It has to do with intelligence. Let the most intelligent people do the strategizing, regardless of their titles.

2. There are no principles. I admit I haven't read many books on planning (or any, for that matter) but in my interviews and conversations with planners I always ask the same question—what are the principles of account planning? I never get the same answer twice. All I get is baloney and jargon about branding and engagement and conversations and the voice of the consumer. A discipline with no principles is not a discipline—it's an amusement.

3. It has encroached on the authority of creative directors. Although nobody in an ad agency has perfect pitch, one would hope that a creative director would have extraordinary insights into motivating consumers. In many agencies, however, creative directors have become supplicants who need permission from planners. Are there talented planners who are invaluable to some creative directors? Of course. But for the most part, planners are inserting themselves into areas where they have no business going.

4. Planning has degraded account service. In agencies with large planning departments, account managers have become little more than project managers. We used to be able to attract talented marketed people to our account services departments because they had substantial strategic responsibilities. Fewer talented marketing people choose to work in an account services department anymore because their strategic responsibilities have been devalued.

5. There is no evidence that it works. Throw out the previous four reasons and we're still left with a compelling reason to get rid of it—after more than 20 years, there's no evidence that it works. I have seen no reliable studies that indicate that advertising produced with the benefit of planning is any more effective than advertising produced without it. (If you've got some, please send it to me and I promise I'll change my mind.) If clients are to be believed, advertising has actually become less effective in recent years—in direct correlation with the ascendancy of account planning.

Account planning has done its job. It's helped us wrestle control of consumer insights away from client-side research departments. Now it's time to move on.

Do we need research and data? Absolutely. Do we need reliable information about consumer behavior? Absolutely. Do we need people who can synthesize insightful strategies? Absolutely. Do we need amateur anthropo-psycho-sociologists? No thank you.

We need a discipline for developing advertising and brand strategy that is...

    a) based on recognizable principles

    b) not tainted with pseudo-science

    d) verifiable

I don't know what that is, but it certainly ain't planning.

REWRITING HISTORY

Here at *The Ad Contrarian* World Headquarters, one of the great amusements of the past year has been watching the pundit digerati backpedaling and rewriting history.

It now seems that a few years ago when the New Age marketing apostles were yapping about the death of the 30-second spot and the impending demise of television they didn't really mean it.

Joseph Jaffe in "Life After the 30-Second Spot," 2005:
". . . now is the time to come out of my closet with this emphatic statement: The thirty-second spot—at least as it exists today—is either dead, dying, or has outlived its usefulness. Take your pick."

Joseph Jaffe on *The BeanCast*, 2011:
". . . what I wrote about in "Life After the 30-Second Spot". . . I said of course television works, I mean, that's not the issue . . ."

The cause of this revisionism is the amazing resilience of TV and TV advertising in spite of the rapid growth of online advertising.

The Wall Street Journal, yesterday: "Demand Builds for TV Ad Time. As rising gasoline prices and stubbornly high unemployment hold back the U.S. economy, one marketplace still appears to be as hot as ever: TV advertising . . ."

eMarketer, March 29, 2011: "2010 brought a major recovery in TV spending . . . with 9.7% growth . . . said eMarketer CEO and co-founder Geoff Ramsey. "While the growth of online advertising has been robust, it hasn't stopped brand advertisers from keeping the bulk of their budgets flowing through TV sets."

Thinkbox, January 27, 2011: "According to new figures from the Broadcasters' Audience Research Board (BARB), in 2010 the average (UK) TV viewer watched 28 hours, 15 minutes of live, linear TV a week (4 hours, 2 minutes a day). This is an increase of 2 hours,

4 minutes a week (18 minutes a day) on 2009 and represents an all time high in TV viewing."

The New York Times, December 6, 2010:

"The success story, perhaps surprisingly, has been television," said Steve King, chief executive at the ZenithOptimedia media division of the Publicis Groupe. TV is, by his estimates, still gaining share of the overall advertising market . . . to 40.7 percent in 2010, from 37 percent in 2005."

So now we're getting a new version of history.

According to the new version, what the advertising experts actually meant was that online advertising wasn't really going to destroy everything in its path. The new orthodoxy is that online advertising is just another tool in our toolbox. You know, kinda like door hangers or hooter wobblers. And the way to use it properly is as part of a media mix along with traditional advertising.

They never meant to imply that other forms of advertising were obsolete or outdated. Or dead, or dying, or had outlived their usefulness.

Oh, heck, no. Our bad.

It was just idiots like us who misunderstood what they were saying when they said things like this:

"The post-advertising age is under way . . . the present is apocalyptic. Any hope for a seamless transition—or any transition at all—from mass media and marketing to micro media and marketing are absurd." Bob Garfield, *Ad Age,* 2009.

". . . there's plenty of bad economic news floating around. From the price of oil to Wall Street to bailouts to the death of traditional advertising." Seth Godin, 2008

". . . the writing is on the wall . . . at the end of the day, people want to consume content without the friction of having to sit down in front of a television at an appointed time . . . People want to see the whole show on YouTube. There is a fundamental shift in consumer behavior going on . . ." From *TechCrunch,* November 2006, "Let's Just Declare TV

Dead And Move On"

" *Traditional TV won't be here in seven to 10 years . . . It's changing so fast that I don't know if it's even going to be that long.* " From *Wired*, April 2007: "The TV Is Dead. Long Live The TV"

"*One of the founding fathers of the internet has predicted the end of traditional television . . . Vint Cerf, who helped to build the internet . . . said . . . that viewers would soon be downloading most of their favourite programmes onto their computers.* " From *The Telegraph*, 2007: TV Is Dying Says Google Expert

You see, these people didn't really mean that TV, and traditional advertising were dead, they just meant . . . uh, you know . . . pizza tastes really good.

Yeah, yeah, that's what they meant.

IS BILL GATES STILL STUNNED?

From *FoxNews.com,* January 2007 . . .

Bill Gates: Internet Will Revolutionize Television

DAVOS, Switzerland - The Internet is set to revolutionize television within five years, due to an explosion of online video content and the merging of PCs and TV sets, Microsoft chairman Bill Gates said on Saturday.

"I'm stunned how people aren't seeing that with TV, in five years from now, people will laugh at what we've had."

Well, Bill, your 5 five years are up. I don't hear any laughing.

The untold story of the past ten years is how astonishingly powerful television has been. Despite all the predictions of its demise, television viewing is stronger than ever.

- TV viewership has grown between 9% and 20% since 2000 (depending on whose numbers you like best)
- 99% of all video viewing is still done on a television. 1% is done on a computer
- TiVo and all other DVR devices account for only 5–6% of viewing
- TiVo has had no discernible effect on ad effectiveness or consumer buying behavior
- According to The Economist, self-reported tales of "I never watch tv anymore" are mostly baloney
- TV viewership is at its highest point ever in history

As we have said many times, marketers always overestimate the appeal of new things and always underestimate the power of traditional consumer behavior.

And here's a little inside info for the next web maniac who's planning to write about the death of TV: People like it.

WHY WE NEED TO KILL THEM ALL

On a number of occasions I've said we need to kill all account planners and start over. Here's why.

Last week they had a big hoo-hah account planning conference in Miami (missed it—had to wash my hair.)

Ad Age ran a column about the high points. The conclusions from this conference are so mind-numbingly dumb that they are almost a parody of themselves.

Here are a few choice excerpts along with some comments from Yours Truly:

"People are no longer waiting to hear from us."

When, I'd like to know, were people waiting to hear from us? Was I sick that week? Advertising is a nuisance. Always has been, always will be. That's why we get the big bucks—to make people pay attention to stuff they're trying desperately to avoid.

"It's a shifting world, and understanding the landscape is more important than ever."

When has the world not been shifting? When have you not had to understand the landscape?

"Understand the conversation, insert your brand into it and then keep going."

You knew it was coming. The fucking "conversation." Will someone PLEASE find a new cliche. The next person I hear say "conversation" is going to die. I'm not kidding.

"We must create content that changes the world."

How about creating content that sells some shit. Wanna change the world? Join the fucking U.N.

It took 650 account planners to come up with this nonsense.

TOP 10 DOUBLE-SECRET UNKNOWN FACTS
ABOUT ADVERTISING

As all *AdContras* know, the marketing and advertising industries have been hijacked by web-addled digi-maniacs who don't know a fact from a fart.

Those of us who like to operate our businesses on the basis of facts, not "buzz" and baloney, are in an ongoing state of war with web marketing hustlers and their endless feedback loop of misleading information.

So, as a service to my loyal, long-suffering *AdContras,* I have put together the *Top 10 Double-Secret Unknown Facts About Advertising.* It is a little crib-sheet to help you fight the forces of ignorance and trendiness wherever you may find them.

Top 10 Double-Secret Unknown Facts About Advertising

1.   99.9% of people who are served an online display ad *do not click* on it.

2.   TV viewership is now at its *highest point ever.*

3.   96% of all retail activity is done in a store. 4% is done online.

4.   DVR owners watch *live TV* 95% of the time. 5% of the time they watch recorded material.

5.   99% percent of all video viewing is done *on a television.* 1% is done on ine.

6.   The difference in purchasing behavior between people who use TiVo and those who don't: *None.*

7.   Since the 1990s, click-through rates for banner ads have *dropped* 97.5%.

8. Since the introduction of TiVo, real time TV viewing has *increased* over 20%.

9. Baby boomers dominate 94% of all consumer packaged goods categories. 5% of advertising is aimed at them.

10. TV viewers are *no more likely* to leave the room during a commercial break than they are before or after the break.

Sources:
1. DoubleClick, Benchmark Report, 2009
2. Nielsen Three Screen Report, Q1 2010;
3. U.S. Department of Commerce, Q2 2010; Nielsen Three Screen Report, Q1 2010
4. Duke University, Do DVRs Influence Sales?
5. Nielsen Three Screen Report, Q1 2010
6. Duke University, Do DVRs Influence Sales?
7. Li, Hairong; Leckenby, John D. (2004). "Internet Advertising Formats and Effectiveness". Center for Interactive Advertising. And DoubleClick, Benchmark Report, 2009
8. NielsenWire, Nov. 10, 2009
9. Marketing Daily, July 22, 2010
10. Council for Research Excellence, May 10, 2010

Date of this post was Sept. 16, 2010

JUNK RESEARCH, SHABBY JOURNALISM,
AND SOCIAL MEDIA

Recently, a colleague sent me an article from *Fast Company* called "What Women Want: Facebook Ads!"

The article was about the amazing ability of Facebook to influence female consumers.

"Businesses may have once had to guess how their ads are being received, but no longer . . . "

. . . is how *Fast Company* put it.

At first glance, the article offers a pretty impressive array of statistics about the power of marketing to women by using Facebook.

On second and third glance, however, it is a very cynical document. It's a terrible example of boosterism disguised as journalism, and self-serving manipulation masquerading as research.

Here are some of the quotes from the *Fast Company* article:

"Half of the respondents said they bought a product in 2009 because of something they'd seen on a social networking site."

". . . a whopping 80% of the women polled said they had (become fans of brands or products)"

". . . it is excellent data for retailers searching for clues about competing in this pinched consumer world."

Well, this is pretty convincing stuff. And there was more. So I decided to explore a little further.

As the source of its information, the *Fast Company* article linked to an article called "Women Warm Up To Brands On Social Sites" on a website called *eMarketer Digital Intelligence.* From this article, I learned that:

"80% of female Internet users said they had become a fan of a product or brand on a social network."

"One-half of female Internet users had brought (sic) a product because of a social network."

Being a semi-open-minded kind of guy, I started thinking that maybe I needed to revise my opinion about the effectiveness of social media marketing.

But something was bothering me. Neither of the articles was very clear about the design or analysis of the research. Who were the women they studied? How were they selected? Who designed the study? Who interpreted the results?

In the case of *Fast Company*, the respondents were characterized as "the women polled" or the "respondents." In *eMarketer*, the respondents were identified as "Internet users."

The article at *eMarketer* attributed the research to *SheSpeaks*, "Annual Social Media Study."

So I went to *SheSpeaks* to find the study. What I found was startling.

Here's what *SheSpeaks* says about itself.

"Our community engagement programs help brands start conversations with target consumers. We introduce your brand to consumers, create and sustain conversations, capture honest and authentic feedback, and identify and nurture brand advocates. We help your brand story become part of her conversations."

In other words, *SheSpeaks* seems to make its living by finding women who are actively engaged in online social activities and signing them up. Then they further encourage these women to use social media tools to advocate for their clients' brands.

And the only women who took part in this "research" were members of *SheSpeaks!*

If you intentionally set out to create a sample skewed to produce a certain result, you couldn't have done better.

There is not a reputable researcher in the world who would use a sample like this to be representative of anything.

How can you possibly study this group—and only this group—and not get results that are hopelessly skewed? The answer is, you can't. It's like doing research on milk consumption by polling dairy farmers.

And yet, in all the reporting I read, and in the study itself, nowhere is it made clear that this group is way outside the profile of average women and the results should not be considered indicative of average behavior.

There is a certain aspect of the social media marketing culture that gives it an aroma of sneaky unreliability. It's like listening to a 16-year old explain how the car got scratched.

The shame is that gullible clients and naive "digital strategists" are being sold this baloney every day.

FIVE MORE THINGS EVERYBODY IS WRONG ABOUT

After about a hundred years in advertising, there are still things that continue to amaze me.

- How much we don't know
- How the business is still driven primarily by legends and rituals
- How specious opinions about advertising become facts when repeated enough times by self-promoting loud-mouths at worthless conferences

A little over a year ago I wrote a piece called "Facts Still Matter: The Death and Life of Television". The thrust of the piece was about the resilience of TV.

In that piece, I quoted a study done at Ball State University. The study was particularly interesting to me because instead of relying on self-reported data (which is the basis of most media studies and is totally unreliable) they followed people around and watched actual behavior.

The results of the study were eye-opening and completely repudiated the claims of the "television is dead/the 30-second spot is dead/the web has changed everything" crowd who have hustled and bullied their way into the forefront of marketing thinking.

More results from this study have been released and they are equally remarkable. Here are some of the findings:

1. The vast majority of viewers don't leave the room or change the channel when the TV program they are watching goes to commercial —"*86% of viewers remain with live TV during commercials . . .*"

2. The rate of channel surfing is essentially the same during commercials as it is programming —"*11% of viewers change channels during the four minutes of TV programming before the commercial break; only 14% change channels during commercials; and 13% change channels in the four-minute period after programming returns.*"

3. The rate of getting up from the room and leaving is essentially identical during the program and during the spots —*"19% change rooms in the four minutes before a commercial break; 20% during; and 21% in the four minutes after programming returns."*

4. The two most prevalent multi-tasking activities that go on during TV watching have nothing to do with the web —*"Concurrent activities are led by "care of another," at 12% in the two minutes prior to and during commercial breaks; and "meal preparation," at 8% . . . "*

5. The rate of multi-tasking does not increase during commercial breaks. In fact, compared to the 2 minutes before a commercial break, multi-tasking actually decreases by 1% during commercials.

Next time some digi-dork vomits up the old "no one watches commercials anymore" line, smack him in the head for me.

VISITING THE LAND OF MAKE-BELIEVE

Today, once again, we visit the land of make-believe.

It's a land that is inhabited by a new species of human being. These new humans are very young and they're very different from us.

- They don't use or believe traditional media.
- They don't like to be marketed to.
- They get their information online, where they develop brand relationships and have conversations with and about brands.
  - They hate advertising.

If you want to reach this new species, you need to throw away all your stupid old assumptions about marketing and advertising.

Only one problem with this wonderful new land—it exists only in the minds of web hustlers and their impressionable followers.

Here are some inconvenient facts:

1. The current generation of teens watches more TV than any other generation in history. TV viewing among teens is up 6% in the last five years.
2. Teens spend less than half as much time on line as the average person.
3. Teens spend 1/3 less time watching online video than adults 25–34.
4. Teens do the following things more than average:

    - Read newspapers
    - Listen to radio
    - Like advertising

Facts seem to have a terrible habit of undermining everything we hear from the people who are constantly chirping at us about the land of make-believe. It might be a good idea to listen to some wise words from the Nielsen people who just released the facts quoted above:

"In media and marketing (there is a) frenetic quest to understand how teens use media, made murky by assumptions that teens somehow behave radically differently than their parents and other consumers . . . Our findings challenge a whole host of assumptions about the media habits of this generation—offering a few surprises as we separate myth from reality."

If you're looking to piss your advertising budget away, a really good idea is to ignore the facts and take a magic carpet ride to never, never land.

It's a land that has been dreamed up by a small coterie of online maniacs and gullible marketers who attend each other's conferences, read each other's blogs and re-tweet each other's inanities.

Caveat emptor, baby.

WHO'S NIELSEN TRYING TO FOOL?

Like most of you, I would like some reliable data about social media that I can take to my clients and say, "Look, social media isn't all hype. Here's some data to show that it really works."

Yesterday I finally thought I had some.

I received an email from Nielsen informing me that they were "releasing the results of an important new study."

The report is called "Understanding the Value of a Social Media Impression" and purports to quantify for us the value of "paid" and "earned" media advertising on Facebook.

Unfortunately, from what I can tell, the report is complete nonsense.

The first thing that caught my eye was this sentence in the email:

"Through our joint partnership with Facebook we are committed to helping marketers fully leverage social media to build their brands."

Right away a red flag went up. Honest researchers aren't "committed" to anything other than reporting the truth. Researchers with agendas and "commitments" aren't doing research, they're doing advocacy.

It just kept getting worse. In the report itself, they state:

"We have now conducted six months of research consisting of . . . more than 125 individual Facebook advertising campaigns from 70 brand advertisers . . . "

The implication is that this study is the result of all that research. Otherwise, why mention it? It's not until four pages later that we learn . . .

"For the purposes of this case study, we examined the impact of Facebook advertising on 14 campaigns . . . Campaigns selected were representative of more successful campaigns . . . "

Huh?

In other words, of the "more than 125 individual Facebook advertising campaigns" they have studied, they only picked 14 of the top performers for this "case study" (and notice how it has mutated from an "important new study" to a "case study" so they have a loophole to crawl through when this baloney hits the fan.)

So, let's recap. You take only the top 11% of the campaigns, you ignore all the failures and all the mediocrities, you analyze only these top performers and you present the results as if they prove something?

"This study demonstrates that advertising in the social context works for brands and works well."

This isn't research. This is a new business pitch.

Chapter 7

The Advertising Follies

SOCIAL MEDIA'S MASSIVE FAILURE

For several years there has been consensus among a very vocal and highly placed group of marketing executives and commentators that fundamental changes have taken place in our culture and in technology which render traditional modes of marketing communication no longer relevant or effective.

The thinking behind the hypothesis goes like this:

- Marketing is a "conversation."
- People are no longer willing to accept the "interruption" model of advertising.
- The objective of marketing communication is for a brand to create "engagement" with consumers.
- Traditional forms of advertising do not create engagement and have substantially outlived their usefulness.
- The Internet has created an environment in which consumer control of his/her purchasing behavior is unprecedented.
- Consumers are quickly moving away from brands that are obviously out to sell them something in favor of brands that seek to engage with them and have conversations.
- Social media represents the most effective medium for engaging with consumers and having these conversations.

Among mainstream brands that have adopted this new marketing paradigm, none has been more zealous than Pepsi-Cola.

Last year, Pepsi substantially abandoned its long-standing commitment to traditional advertising in favor of social media. It canceled its annual Super Bowl advertising. It diverted tens of millions of dollars from traditional advertising to create the "Pepsi Refresh Project." *Pepsi Refresh* was an online social media initiative in which Pepsi gave out 20 million dollars. They also spent many millions more in support of this initiative.

I am pretty certain *Refresh* is the largest social media initiative ever undertaken. Never before, to my knowledge, has a brand taken so much of its traditional advertising money and energy and redirected it into social media.

Most major brands have some kind of social media program. But never before, to my knowledge, has a major consumer brand made a social media program the centerpiece of its advertising and marketing.

"We took the divergent path," explained Frank Cooper, chief consumer engagement officer for Pepsi. "We wanted to explore how a brand could be integrated into the digital space."

The idea behind the program was that you, the consumer, got to engage with Pepsi by voting for the *Refresh* projects you deemed most worthy. There were also other opportunities to engage through an enormous online effort—Facebook, Twitter, YouTube, website, blogs. Millions of dollars were also spent in what might be called "traditional advertising in support of social media."

Skeptics (such as yours truly) have been eagerly awaiting a report card on this initiative as it is the first real test case for a major brand implementing a massive transfer of marketing resources from traditional advertising to social media.

The results are now in. It has been a disaster.

- Last week, *The Wall Street Journal* reported that Pepsi-Cola and Diet Pepsi had each lost about 5% of their market share in the past year.
- If my calculations are correct, for the Pepsi-Cola brand alone this represents a loss of over $350 million. For both brands, the loss is probably something in the neighborhood of 400 million to half-a-billion dollars.
- For the first time ever Pepsi-Cola has dropped from its traditional position as the number two soft drink in America to number three (behind Diet Coke.)

In 2010, Pepsi's market share erosion accelerated by 8 times compared to the previous year.

The *Refresh Project* accomplished everything a social media program is expected to: Over 80 million votes were registered; almost

3.5 million "likes" on the Pepsi Facebook page; almost 60,000 Twitter followers. The only thing it failed to do was sell Pepsi.

It achieved all the false goals and failed to achieve the only legitimate one.

In reaction to this disaster, Massimo d'Amore, chief executive of PepsiCo Americas Beverages had this to say . . .

"When my ancestors went from the Middle Ages to the Renaissance, they blew up the place, so that's what we are doing."

He also said . . .

"We need television to make the big, bold statement . . ."

Social media has taken a huge hit. Only zealots and fools will continue to bow down to the gods of social media.

THE HANDSOMEST MAN IN THE WORLD

That's me. The handsomest.

What? You don't believe me?

I have affidavits from my mother, my wife, and several of my employees.

I have awards from the American Association of Old Fat Bald Guys.

What? You still don't believe? You think I'm lying?

Okay, maybe I'm not really the handsomest. Maybe I'm just trying to make a point.

The point is this. You would think that one of the first things people trained in advertising would learn is that what you *say* can be very different from what you *communicate.*

I can walk into a room and say, "I am the handsomest man in the world." What I am communicating, however, is "I am a great big jerk."

Not one person in the room will believe that I am the handsomest man in the world, and everyone in the room will believe I am a jerk.

When you say something that no one believes, you are not only wasting your money, you are undermining your credibility. And all the spurious "support points" in the world don't make absurd claims any more believable.

Yet advertisers continue to ignore the distinction between what they are saying and what they are communicating.

Electronics retailers continue to talk about their "great customer service." Banks continue to talk about the importance of "relationships." Computer peripheral manufacturers continue to talk about "plug and play."

All they are communicating is that they are bullshit artists who can't be trusted.

BEATING THEIR HEADS AGAINST THE WALL

For several years now, we at *Ad Contrarian* Global Headquarters have been ranting about the astonishing stupidity of marketers for relentlessly chasing young people and ignoring people over 50.

Just to recap the case:

- People over 50 control over 75% of the financial assets of the US.
- Baby boomers dominate 94% of all consumer packaged goods categories.
- They purchase almost 40% of consumer packaged goods
- They account for ⅓ of all TV viewers, online users, social media users and Twitter users
- Even in technology categories, where marketers assume young people dominate, baby boomers "are purchasing at rates just as high as other segments, and because they are often buying for their kids, many are double-dipping."

The astounding part: according to Nielsen, less than 5% of advertising is aimed at people over 50.

Apparently NBC is going to make a big presentation tomorrow to marketers and agencies about how stupid they are for ignoring people over 50. All I can say to NBC is, good luck.

For the past 10 years the lemmings in the marketing world have been trapped between the legends and rituals of the past, and the brave new world of the future. They are too busy jumping from one "thing that will change everything" to another to pay attention to the people who actually spend the world's money. They are too busy developing mobile apps for penniless 16-year olds to focus on the people who control this country economically.

According to NBC . . .

- The 55–64 age group . . . "is the fastest-growing demo group in the country and now numbers 35 million people that account for close to $2 trillion in annual spending."

- Nielsen's demo groups . . . "were invented 50 years ago and are outdated."
- People 55–64 have . . . "a median household income of $69,000, dwarfing that of those under 25 ($27,000) and 25–34 ($58,000) . . ."
- Nielsen doesn't even report the TV viewership of people over 55.

NBC CEO Jeff Zucker said, "What we'd like to see is these companies and their agencies start targeting (the 55–64 group) as much as they do the 18–34 demo . . ."

Yeah. In your dreams.

Anyone who has spent one week in an ad agency knows that facts no longer matter, and the minute you start talking to clients about targeting people over 50 is the minute they start labeling you a "dinosaur."

I recently was at a meeting with a bank at which I tried to explain to them how ridiculous their strategy of targeting young people was. They looked at me like I had 3 heads.

The marketing industry is locked into an out-of-date time warp in which young people are the holy grail.

If anything, it's getting worse

HOW TO BE FABULOUSLY SUCCESSFUL

People often say to me, *"Ad Contrarian,* how can I be a fabulously successful online copywriter like you?"

Well, I'm here to tell you that you, too, can be famous and make millions of dollars and have super-hot nymphos crawling all over you.

What's the secret to online copywriting success? First, you need some words. Words are the building blocks of writing! Without words, writing is a thankless chore. Take the Sumerians. They didn't have words. All they had were pictures. Now they're dead.

The best part? They're all free! Any word you want. Even "penultimate."

When we write online copy, the words we use say a lot about us. If we are depressed, we want to use depressing words like "advertising" or "exercise."

If we are funny, then we want to use funny words, like "homo" or "Kotex."

The important thing is to be yourself when you are writing. You have to know who you really are. If you don't know who you are, you have to find yourself. The best place to find yourself is in bed. Hopefully, with someone cute.

The Key To Being Creative: Creativity

In order to be a successful online copywriter you have to be creative. The most important part of being creative is "creativity". Without "creativity" most of us wouldn't have a creative bone in our body. Except maybe our fibula.

Nobody really knows what "creativity" is. Every year thousands of people take a pilgrimage to find out. This involves flying to Cannes, snorting cocaine, and having sex with smokers.

How do you nourish your creativity? I suggest chicken caesar wraps. But I know a very successful creative director who swears by strawberry Toaster Strudel.

The important thing to remember is that we're all creative. Although, honestly, I have my doubts about Leon Panetta.

The F Word: It's Effing Awesome!

On the internet, content is king. And dirty words is queen.

If you are writing a blog, you must be hard-boiled and never show weakness. You must not let on that you are from Valley Stream and went to Hofstra and worked at Grey. You must show the world that you're an anarchistic, hard-living, hard-drinking bastard. And what better way to be a bad-ass muthafucka than to use naughty language.

Words like "fuck," "bullshit," and "douchebag" make your copy sing! Put a few of them together and you've got magic—"Fuckingdouchebag!," "Fuckingbullshit!," "Fuckingfuck!" (By the way, it is impossible to punctuate that last sentence properly, even for a successful online copywriter.)

The ability to express complex concepts in a censorship-free environment is what makes the web great. Well, that and those nutty cats on YouTube.

Understanding Your Online Customer

Let's face it. Most of the people who visit your website are fuckingdouchebags.

I mean … um … they are Web 2.0 savvy consumers whose engagement with their own personal brands make them willing to join the conversation in an interactive way that leverages social media to become engaged customers for life. You know, that kind of thing.

Well, whatever the hell they are, they got money and we want it!

Remember, engaging content is how you engage their engagement.

The Three Simple, Double-Secret Magical Copywriting Rules for Success
Now we get to the heart of the matter. Anyone can be a successful online copywriter if you just follow these three simple, double-secret, magical rules:

1. Don't use Windex on your computer screen. It fucks up the molecules or something.

2. Don't hold back. People love to know personal details about your life. Unless you have a hernia or some kind of smelly intestinal disorder.

3. Amateur MILF in wild inter-racial 3-way . . . Oops, sorry, wrong blog.

COOKIE MONSTROSITY

One thing you can say about the Internet with absolute certainty—there has never been another medium that has spawned more idiotic ideas.

The latest comes from Pepperidge Farm. From some retro universe they have launched a campaign called *Connecting Through Cookies* (I kid you not.) The centerpiece is a website called *The Art of the Cookie.*

You see, this website is going to be a social network (apparently there aren't enough online social networks) and lonely housewives are going to get together on line and talk about their cookies. And if you think I'm going to make a cheap joke here, I want to remind you that my daughter reads this stuff.

Anyway, the marketing genius behind the idea had this to say . . . the company conducted ethnographic research by "going into our consumers' homes, sitting down with them, talking to them about how they use our products."

Hope you didn't pay too much for that ethnographic research, Mr. Pepperidge—they use your products by *eating them.* No charge.

And, by the way, if there are any lonely housewives out there who want to connect through their cookies, I have a very nice single friend.

ADVERTISING REFLECTS EVERYTHING

In San Francisco we have something called "casual carpools." People line up, you pick them up in your car, and then you can cross the Bay Bridge in the carpool lane.

I once picked up a crazy old lady who thought every license plate had a secret meaning. The whole trip she was trying to interpret license plates. "5JNU361. What do you think that means?"

The advertising press is like that. They think every ad has a significant social context.

So if the economy is lousy, they suddenly notice that there are price ads in the world. If times are good, they brilliantly perceive that luxury goods are for sale.

According to these guys, no matter what is happening in the wider world, it is always reflected in advertising.

In an article entitled, "Down Economic Times Elicit Upbeat Campaigns", *The New York Times* seems to be surprised that in a bad economy advertisers are trying to portray their products in a positive light.

"It seems counterintuitive to accentuate the positive amid all the downbeat financial news."

Really? What are we supposed to say to consumers? You're ugly and this stuff is shit?

WOULDN'T IT BE GREAT

Wouldn't it be great if there were hundreds of different YouTubes?

And they were technologically advanced so the video didn't start and stop and drive you crazy while it was loading and bufffering?

And the content wasn't 99% home-made crap, but was actually professionally done?

And you could watch long-form stuff, like movies?

And you didn't have to fuss with it and waste time searching for stuff?

And, in addition to video, you could see stuff happening in real time?

Wouldn't that be great?

Oh wait a minute.

There is something.

It's called television.

Never mind.

SIDEWALK PSYCHIATRY

One of these day I'm going to write a book about the demise of advertising.

It will start like this:

Once upon a time, advertising people decided that they no longer wanted to sell things. Instead, they decided it would be more fun to be amateur psychoanalysts. And so, instead of making ads about the attributes of the products they were selling, they started making ads about the imagined psychological profiles of their customers.

I was reading an article from *USA Today* recently about a new ad campaign for a large company whose name I'm not going to tell you yet.

The reason I'm not going to tell you is that I want you to look at the target definition and tell me if you can figure out what these people are selling. Or even what category they are competing in. Presumably a target definition is something specific and relevant to the product you're peddling. Otherwise, why do it?

". . . we focus on a target audience based on a psychographic profile. Our target . . . is the everyday hero and they share five core values: family first, work-life balance, self knowledge and fulfillment, spirit of independence and fun and enjoyment. The other thing we know about (them) is they take great pride in staying true to themselves.."

I've seen this exact same baloney on about a thousand creative briefs. What it really means is, our target audience is just like our account planners.

So here's what I want to know. Who are they not targeting? Who doesn't . . .

- put family first
- want work-life balance
- seek self-knowledge and fulfillment
- have a spirit of independence
- seek fun and enjoyment.
- take great pride in staying true to themselves

If you're a creative and you want to do good work, the only way to deal with nonsense like this is to burn it. Then try to find something interesting to say about the product.

Next, what do you think these people are selling? Cars? Lipstick? Golf clubs? Running shoes? Clothing? Beer? Vitamin water? Organic foods? Life insurance? Underwear?

The company is Holiday Inn.

Here's some free advice. I've been to a Holiday Inn recently. I didn't see too many people wandering around looking for "self-knowledge and fulfillment."

Mostly they were looking for clean towels and a bucket of ice.

THE ABSURDITY OF WHAT WE DO

This is a true story about the absurdity of advertising.

I was once creative director of an ad agency that had offices with a lovely view of San Francisco Bay.

One of our accounts was the Matson shipping line. The shipping line was doing something amazing with one of its ships and they wanted us to create an ad about it.

They were going to take an enormous cargo ship and lengthen it. First, an army of workmen with blowtorches were going to cut the ship in half. Then they were going to add an entire new section between the two halves. Then they were going to weld the whole thing back together. Then they would repaint and refurbish the ship. And then they would relaunch it. It was a monumental undertaking.

The day the work began one of our art directors, Genji Handa, flew down to the shipyard in Long Beach, CA to shoot photographs of the workmen beginning the, literally, titanic job of cutting this ship in half.

The photos were taken. Later the retouching was done. Then the copy was written. The layouts were sent to the client. The client ad manager had comments, the comments were addressed, the copy was re-written.

The ad was circulated throughout the client organization. Advertising being what it is, others at the client had comments. The ad was re-written and re-laid out, it was sent back to the ad manager. More changes were made . . .

One afternoon, Genji was sitting in his office working on what he hoped was the final iteration of the ad. He looked out his window. Coming through the Golden Gate into San Francisco Bay was the ship.

They finished making the ship before we finished making the ad.

LET'S SAVE PEPSI 10 MILLION

Here at *The Ad Contrarian* World Headquarters, we are sometimes accused of being too negative. Of course, nothing could be farther from the truth. Nonetheless, as Marvin Gaye once famously said, "we're all sensitive people."

Consequently, we've decided to do something positive for our friends over at Pepsi. Their Pepsi *Refresh* project may have turned out to be a pig's breakfast for them, but it's been a source of great material for us. And we'd like to thank them by giving them a gift of 10 million dollars.

So we gathered all the marketing professionals here at TAC World Headquarters together, and said, "We'd like to give our friends at Pepsi a gift. We need a marketing idea that's worth $10 million. Who's got one?"

We decided to call it the Pepsi *Replenish* project. We worked on it all week (okay, fifteen minutes) and today we are proud to announce the winning idea.

Before we do I'm afraid we're going to have to start with a little math. It's copywriter math—always a dicey proposition—but necessary in this case. We figure the Pepsi *Refresh* project cost Pepsi at least $40 to $50 million last year.

And what did they get for their $40 million? Well, let's see . . . they lost 5% of their market share . . . they dropped to third place in their category . . . hmm . . . oh, yeah . . . they got about 3 million Faceboogers to say they "like" Pepsi. Fantastic!

As every social media expert will avow, that's a fabulous success and a brilliant use of marketing dollars. Well, believe it or not, the Pepsi Replenish project has unearthed an even brillianter idea.

Next year, Mr. Pepsi, cancel all the media, take down all the websites, tear up all the marketing materials, fire all the marketing experts, and send some interns out onto the street with ten dollar bills.

They can give a $10 bill to anyone who promises to "like" Pepsi.

After they've handed out 3 million $10 bills, you will have achieved the same level of fantastic success as last year—another 3 million people who "like" you. But this time, it will cost you only $30 million instead of $40 million—a savings of $10 million!

And the best part is the 3 million people you give the 10 bucks to won't just say they like you, they *really will* like you. And, who knows, this time they might even use the money to buy some Pepsi.

THE JUSTIFICATION BUSINESS

Advertising today consists of two very different disciplines: Making ads and making the justification for ads.

The way ad agencies work (especially the big ones) is that most of the effort is spent making the justification for the ads—research, planning, brand analysis, meetings, presentations, strategy sessions, briefs, conference calls, downloads, uploads, deep dives, off sites and insights followed by revised research, planning, brand analysis, meetings, presentations, strategy sessions, briefs, conference calls, downloads, uploads, deep dives, off sites and insights.

After months of this stuff, when all the knuckleheads are satisfied that justification has been achieved, as a byproduct of all this activity, sometimes an ad appears somewhere.

Justification has become the business. Ads have become the byproduct.

FINALLY, THE TRUE VALUE OF A FACEBOOK FAN

In days of yore, people were consumed by questions about the nature of God, or the origin of the universe, or the search for the Holy Grail. Today, however, we face a problem that is apparently even more vexing: What the heck is the value of a Facebook fan?

Based on the alarming amount of literature on the topic, this seems to be very nettlesome to today's highly sensitive marketing professionals.

I've been studying the methods of our industry's new oracles— the data analysts—and trying to apply their methods and their logic to the problem.

And, good news. I think I've got the answer!

Here's what I've done. I've used real-world numbers, based on a real-world case history and come up with what I believe is an unassailable value for a Facebook fan.

I have tried to keep this mainstream by using one of the most famous brands in the world, and a very famous Facebook initiative to derive my value.

The formula I've used is a simple one highly favored by our data wizards. I've taken the total change in dollar sales since the Facebook program in question began, and I've divided it by the total number of Facebook fans that were acquired. That should give us a dollar value for each Facebook fan.

The case history I'm going to use is the Pepsi *Refresh* Project. According to Pepsi's marketing director "the success has been overwhelming" so no one can accuse me of skewing the data.

The Pepsi Facebook page has acquired about 3.5 million fans as a result of the *Refresh* project. In the most recent year, during which the *Refresh* Project was ongoing, Pepsi sales dropped by about 350 million dollars.

Doing the math, we find that each Pepsi Facebook fan was worth about 100 dollars.

To Coke.

Chapter 8

Contrariana

THE LEGEND OF MARKETING MAN

Basically, there are two types of men—Feckless Weasels and Smelly Hairballs.

Your classic Feckless Weasel lives in Berkeley, drives a Subaru Outback, spends 80% of his time trying to please his shrill harridan of a wife, and wastes the other 20% of his life "reasoning" with his horrid children ("Now, Joshie, you remember we said that in a restaurant you shouldn't put your feet in other peoples' food . . .")

The Smelly Hairball has old banana peels in his golf bag, is at least three months behind in his alimony, has an expired driver's license and is quite fond of the phrase "I said, *shut the fuck up!*"

In the rich pageant of manhood there is, sadly, very little fertile ground between the Feckless Weasel and the Smelly Hairball.

There is, however, one exception—Marketing Man.

Marketing Man is an imaginary character (or as we like to call him, a "target audience") who exists mainly in ad agency briefing documents and marketing department Powerpoint presentations.

Marketing Man is handsome and well-groomed. He is thoughtful and considerate. He is a close shaver. He coaches soccer and is concerned with his wife's feelings. He is helpful in the kitchen and undemanding in the bedroom. He keeps his closet neat and his weenie in his pants. In other words, he's a total fucking dork.

Well, Marketing Man now has an online place all to himself where he can gather with other Marketing Men and have conversations about . . . oh, I don't know . . . sauces?

It's a super-slick website called *Man Of The House* sponsored by P&G. It's billed as "a man's guide to grooming, gadgets, fitness, relationships, clothes, parenting, careers & home repair." That's right, everything that makes contemporary life such a total pile of crap. (Couldn't they put in just a little about strippers, weed, and golf? Just a little?)

Here are some of the things you can learn this week at *Man Of The House:*

- *Tips for Surviving a Weekend at Disney*
- *What Does Your Wife Want From You?*
- *4 Reasons Not To Tuck Your Shirt In*
- *How to Clean a Toilet in 30 Seconds Flat*

Hemingway is spinning.

FIVE ETERNAL, IMMUTABLE LAWS OF ADVERTISING

1. Whoever controls the research wins.
2. The smaller the account, the larger the committee.
3. The acquirer is always dumber than the acquiree.
4. The dumbest person in your agency will someday be your client.
5. The hotter the climate, the colder the meeting room.

THE YELLOW AND BROWN PROCESS

Prospective clients want to believe that there is a method to the madness.

More and more, success in winning new clients is not about the effectiveness of the advertising you create, but about how clever you are at back-filling a convincing process behind your creative endeavors.

Well, there are processes for doing just about everything an agency does. But when it comes to creating ideas, sorry, there ain't no process. I once asked marketing icon Jack Trout how much of his success was due to his process and how much to inspiration. He said 95% inspiration.

Don't get me wrong, we all pretend there's a process. We have to. Clients insist. We sometimes even give it a name . . . oops, sorry . . . I mean, we brand it.

A prospective client once asked me what process I used to create an ad he particularly liked. I told him I used the "Yellow and Brown" process. He seemed excited, "Really? What's the 'Yellow and Brown' process?"

"I took a legal pad with me to the bathroom."

We didn't get the account.

WHEN WHITE PEOPLE RUN WILD

My daughter goes to school in Portland, Oregon and I've been spending some time there.

Portland is a lovely city with nice people. But it's an extreme case of what happens when white people are allowed to run wild without the palliative effect of other races.

First you notice that there are way too many bicycles clogging up the roads. And that every bicycle rider has one of those pointy-headed space-age helmets even though they're traveling at an infuriating 4 miles an hour.

Tattoos are apparently required by law, as are facial piercings. These often serve as personality substitutes.

Everything is either sustainable or said to be so (note to overly-fervent environmentalists: The second law of thermodynamics predicts that the universe is subject to something called *entropy*, which is pretty solid confirmation that *nothing* is sustainable. But we'll leave that for another day.)

And speaking of sustainability, citizens of Portland seem to have unrealistically high confidence in the resiliency of their lung tissue, as they smoke cigarettes with alarming enthusiasm.

The most successful enterprises in Portland appear to be second-hand clothing stores, second-hand furniture stores, and second-hand food carts.

Of course, the Northwest coffee fetish is well-established and there seems to be a coffee shop-to-inhabitant ratio of 3-to-1.

Now don't get me wrong. I like Portland, and some of my best friends are white. It's just that these people actually put pineapple on their pizza. This is an abomination that a more diverse citizenry would never abide.

Fashion Tips For Portlanders:

For gals: Unless you're headed to women's volleyball practice, sweatpants in the evening are a fashion no-no. Take a look around you. Sweatpants are mostly the domain of fat guys with disagreeable rashes.

For guys: Your soul patch is way too big. It shouldn't be covering your entire chin. Check out Dizzy Gillespie. This is the way you wear a soul patch. I know you're trying to look like a hip jazz player, but you look more like a clueless relief pitcher.

(This piece pre-dated "Portandia". Just sayin'. . . B.H.)

WHAT THEY SAY AND WHAT THEY MEAN

There are two kinds of ad clients.

The first kind is the good kind. They speak in plain English and give simple, clear direction.

Then there is the second kind. They're watching a channel we don't get. They speak a language we don't understand.

It sounds and looks like English but it's not. It has vowels and consonants just like English, but somehow they don't work the same way. They use the same words we use, but they mean different things.

It's kind of like looking at a toothbrush and finding out it's called a hat.

In our ongoing effort to explain the world of advertising to our thoughtful and charming readers, the staff here at TAC has taken it upon itself to create a little guide book that will help you understand what those "Type 2" clients mean when they are talking to you about advertising.

- When they say, "We need to make an emotional connection with the consumer" they mean, "Put a one-legged marathoner in the spot."

- When they say, "I don't see how this differentiates us" they mean, "Add some bullshit about quality and value."

- When they say, "Does this carry enough branding?" they mean, "Make the logo bigger."

- When they say, "Will this ad stand out?" they mean, "Make the product shot bigger."

- When they say, "We need a more holistic approach" they mean, "I just met with a social media expert. Make a Facebook page."

- When they say, "Have you thought of any non-traditional elements?" they mean, "Do something with mobile phones."

- When they say, "We need to thoroughly re-evaluate our brand architecture" they mean, "Our ceo just met with a branding consultant, get ready for a three month Powerpoint fest."
- When they say, "We need to evaluate all our marketing resources" they mean, "You're fired."

PHILOSOPHY OR DONUTS?

Several years ago, a very sincere guy who ran a chain of donut shops came to see me. He wanted to do an advertising campaign.

"We're different," he explained. "We're a commune. Everyone who works here owns an equal part. We work cooperatively. It's a model for how businesses should be run. It's a vision of the future. I think people will really respond to this if we do an advertising campaign about it."

"How are your donuts?" I asked.

"Good."

"Then forget the philosophy. Nobody needs more philosophy. They need good donuts."

DOES MARKETING MAKE YOU STUPID?

It's amazing how quickly otherwise intelligent people become knuckleheads when exposed to marketing.

I am often invited by clients to attend confabs about sales and marketing. Over the years I have met many staff members of these client organizations. Some have been in sales, some in operations, some in finance, some in manufacturing.

As many corporations will do, these people are often moved out of one area and into another. A smart sales person who is moved to manufacturing remains smart. A smart finance person who is moved to operations remains smart. But take someone out of any other department and put her in marketing, and she immediately becomes a jargon-monkey.

Suddenly, someone who used to have intelligent things to say is overcome by the compulsion to spout nothing but cliches.

Instead of talking about getting further information, she now talks about "deep dives."

Instead of dates, she now has "time frames."

All of a sudden her vocabulary is limited to "low-hanging fruit" and "messaging" and "engagement" and "hand-raisers" and, of course, "conversations."

What's going on here? Does marketing make you stupid? Can't you speak like a human anymore?

Or is marketing an occupation that is so shallow and so obsessed with trendiness that you can't feel comfortable unless you think and sound just like everyone else?

OPENING DAY

The economy is in the toilet. The ad industry is a disaster. Asteroids are heading toward Earth. Web pornography is warping the minds of our children. Grown men and women are relentlessly Tweeting each other.

Yes, my friend, the end is near.

But who gives a shit?

It's Opening Day. I'm going to have a hot dog and a beer. I'm going to sit in the sunshine till the back of my neck is red and raw and my ass stings like a shot of tequila on a bad patch of strep throat.

What the hell, I'm having two hot dogs.

Once a year, every aspect of life should have an Opening Day. Every business should have one. Every friendship should have one. Every family should have one.

A day when everything starts over. When all of last year's successes and failures go into the record book. A day when the slate is clean and the possibilities are unlimited. A day when you call in sick-and-tired; when you leave the fucking Blackberry in the glove compartment; when you go somewhere where the grass is perfect and the people are unaccountably cheerful.

It's Opening Day. Play ball!

HOW TO ANNOY 40,000 PEOPLE

I am a sports fan and a patriot. I go to many sporting events. But if I have to sit through one more excruciating interpretation of *The Star Spangled Banner* I may never go back.

If you are ever asked to sing the national anthem at a ballgame please follow these simple guidelines:

1. Sing the melody. Songs have melodies for a reason. Your improvisations are not improvements. Trust me on this.

2. Don't gargle. This isn't *American Idol*.

3. There's a difference between drunkenness and admiration. You know all those morons who are going "Wooo!" when you hit the high note? They're drunk.

4. And most of all, get on with it. Patriotism is fine, but our hot dogs are getting cold.

A DEAD KIND OF CAR COMPANY. A DEAD KIND OF CAR.

Advertising that is really good gives you a reason to prefer a product when there is no reason.

That's what Hal Riney did with Saturn.

He took a mediocre vehicle from a sclerotic manufacturer, and brilliantly turned it into a desirable quantity. He did it with his unique blend of plain-talk, humor, beauty, and bullshit.

At one point Saturn had owners from all over the country driving to Spring Hill, Tennessee just to be with other Saturn owners.

He did what all the smarmy brand babblers talk about but never come close to accomplishing—creating a brand. And he did it without once uttering the word "branding." He did it with great ads.

On Friday *The New York Times* reported that Saturn was essentially dead. Since January 1st, Saturn dealerships have closed in 45 cities, while GM, typically, can't figure out what the hell to do with the brand.

In fact, Saturn was dead the day they fired Riney. He understood the brand better than the imbeciles who paid him and ultimately released him. He had to—he invented it.

Great advertising cannot survive the stupidity of large corporations unless there is someone at the top keeping the ignorant jackals at bay. The day the head moron at Saturn let the dogs loose on Riney, the game was over.

If ad agencies had had any integrity, when Saturn went shopping for a new agency, they would have said, "We're not pitching. Here's our advice. You have one valuable asset and one only. It's your advertising. Change it and you will die."

TOP 10 BULLSHIT PROFESSIONS

I was thinking that maybe advertising was the world's number one bullshit profession.

After semi-painstaking analysis and consideration, however, I am happy to report that advertising is way down at number eight.

To develop this list I did two things. First I eliminated all occupations that are obviously scams—like palm reader, astrologer, and economist.

Second, I used only one criterion in creating the list:

Do they really know anything or are they just making shit up?

Okay, drum roll ...

The Ad Contrarian Top 10 Bullshit Professions:

1. Career Counselors: If they knew anything they'd find *themselves* better jobs.

2. Clergymen: God-bothering bullies masquerading as holy men.

3. Psychotherapists: Practitioners of the world's most advanced form of pseudoscience.

4. Politicians: Insufferable egotists pretending to be "public servants."

5. Branding Consultants: Why didn't I think of this scam?

6. Art Critics: Thankfully, no one pays attention except rich twits.

7. Actors: We tell them where to stand. We tell them what to say. They win awards.

8. Ad Executives: You can build a career by memorizing 10 cliches.

9. Financial Advisors: Monkeys throwing darts.

10. Third Base Umpires: One call a game if you're lucky.

BIG BROTHER HAS ARRIVED AND HE'S US

One of the frightening things about human behavior is that horrific social practices are often only recognized as such from a distance.

Practices like slavery, binding of feet and infanticide—which seem perfectly monstrous to us—seemed normal to most of the people in the societies that practiced them. It took time and distance for societies to accept the cruelty and hideousness of these practices.

The same is true of less outrageous, but still odious social customs like segregation, disenfranchisement—even smoking on airplanes.

It's often only with the perspective of time that we realize how wrong social behaviors can be. We're living through such a period now.

The essence of freedom and democracy is being undermined. We can't see it, but it's all around us. It's that "fish can't see the ocean" thing. What's threatening our freedom is tracking on the Internet.

The Internet now knows everything about us. It knows where we go, who we talk to, what we talk about, what and who we like and don't like. It knows what we buy and why we buy it. It knows what we sell and who we sell it to. It knows our names, our addresses, our phone numbers, our credit card numbers, our bank and brokerage accounts. It knows how much money we have, where we keep it and what we do with it. It knows our locations at any moment and whom we are with.

It knows our political beliefs and our sexual habits. It knows what we eat and whether we drink too much. It knows what we think of our bosses and what our bosses think of us. It knows our salaries and our payment histories. It knows what airlines we fly, what cars we buy and what hotels we stay at. It knows what our ailments are, what drugs we use, what doctors we see and what our psychological profiles are.

It relentlessly collects this information 24 hours a day, 365 days a year. It keeps this information in flimsy warehouses where anyone with time or ingenuity can find anything they want to know about us.

It pretends the information is secure, but only a blind fool believes this. It tells us that privacy is an old-fashioned, out-of-date concept. It is reassuring in its pervasiveness.

Then it sells the information to the highest bidder. And sometimes to any bidder at all.

And why does it do all this? For us. For the marketing and advertising industries.

There's no reasonable way that this is a good development for a free society. There is no realistic vision of the future in which this will not lead to appalling mischief.

It's time for us to say no. It's time to put aside our petty self-interest, take a step back and see where this is leading. We need to stop tracking people and their behavior now.

Big Brother has arrived, and he's us.

THE TALKATIVE CHILD

Since Sunday was Father's Day, and I'm sick to death of writing about advertising, I thought I would serve up a little Father' Day reminiscence.

My daughter was a very talkative child. In fact, when we went on car trips it was not unusual for her to talk non-stop for 3 hours. Anyone with a motor-mouthed child knows that this is not an exaggeration.

One day we were on such a trip—my wife and I in the front seat, my 5-year-old daughter in the back in her car seat. We were about 45-minutes into one of her relentless monologues, when suddenly the question popped-up: "Mommy, where do babies come from?"

We looked at each other, gave the nod, took a deep breath, and dived right in.

We told her about eggs and sperm and penises going into vaginas. She received this information in stunned silence.

Then came the kicker. We told her about how she was special. How, because of some medical issues, the doctor had to take the eggs from mommy and the sperm from daddy and put them together in a dish and then put the fertilized egg back into mommy.

Now she was totally lost in thought. You could almost hear the wheels spinning and smell the synapses burning.

One minute went by, silence.

Two minutes went by, silence,

Five minutes went by, silence.

Finally she spoke.

"Mom," she said.

"Yes?" replied my wife.

"I'm so glad you didn't have to do it the regular way."

Acknowledgements

I'd like to thank some people for their help and/or inspiration in the writing of this book. First to Marcie Judelson and Jay Tannenbaum for their honest appraisals when all I really wanted were compliments. To Sharon Krinsky whose ideas inspired several of the pieces — and whose potential ridicule made a lot of them better. To Mike Chapman who recruited me to write some of these pieces for *Adweek*. To Miles Turpin and Martha Abbene for their help in design and production. To the readers of *The Ad Contrarian* blog whose approbation I have in mind every time I turn on my laptop. Finally, to Maria and Lucy for everything.

About the Author

Bob Hoffman is CEO of Hoffman|Lewis advertising in San Francisco and St. Louis. Bob is former CEO of MOJO USA and ex-President and Creative Director of Allen & Dorward. He has served as President of the San Francisco Advertising Club and been on the board of the Advertising and Marketing International Network. Bob was also a middle school science teacher. Bob has created advertising for McDonald's, Toyota, Shell, Nestle, Blue Cross, Chevrolet, Pepsico, Bank of America, Seagrams, and more companies than he cares to remember. Bob is author of the book *The Ad Contrarian* and the blog of the same name. In 2012 he was named "Advertising Person of the Year" by the San Francisco Ad Club.